Hartford Courant.

EXCELLENCE³

**UCONN HUSKIES'
2003-04 WOMEN'S
CHAMPIONSHIP SEASON**

Sports Publishing L.L.C.
www.sportspublishingllc.com

Publisher
Peter L. Bannon

Senior Managing Editors
Joseph J. Bannon Jr. and Susan M. Moyer

Coordinating Editor
Noah A. Amstadter

Developmental Editors
Erin Linden-Levy and Dean Miller

Art Director
K. Jeffrey Higgerson

Copy Editor
Cynthia L. McNew

Book Design
Christine Mohrbacher

Cover Design
Kenneth J. O'Brien

Project Managers, Book Layout
Tracy Gaudreau and Jim Henehan

Imaging
Kenneth J. O'Brien, Kerri Baker,
Dustin Hubbart and Christine Mohrbacher

Hartford Courant.

President, Publisher and Chief Executive Officer
Jack W. Davis Jr.

Senior Vice President and Editor
Brian Toolan

Managing Editor
Clifford L. Teutsch

Deputy Managing Editor
G. Claude Albert

Deputy Managing Editor
Barbara T. Roessner

Associate Editor
Cheryl A. Magazine

Sports Editor
Jeff Otterbein

Assistant Managing Editor/Photo
and Graphics
Thom McGuire

Director of Photography
John Scanlan

Soft cover ISBN: 1-58261-901-8
Hard cover ISBN: 1-58261-902-6

Front Cover Photos by Michael McAndrews/The Hartford Courant
Back Cover Photo by Tia Ann Chapman/The Hartford Courant

Contents

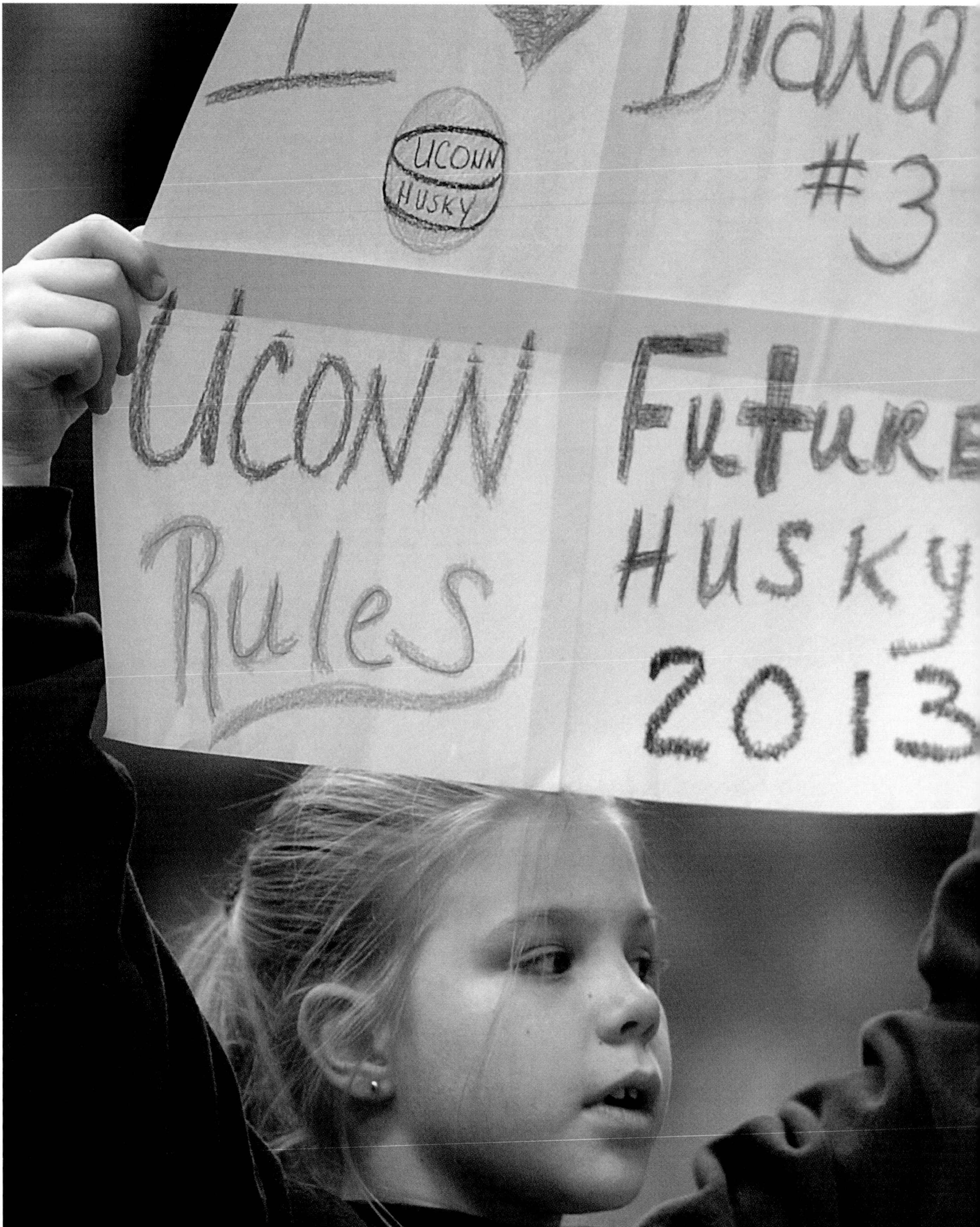
I
Diana
#3
UCONN
HUSKY
UCONN
Rules
Future
HUSKY
2013

ABOVE: The Huskies' mascot entertains the crowd during the first round of the NCAA Tournament.
John Dunn/Icon SMI

LEFT: A young fan shows her support for Diana Taurasi and the UConn Huskies during the Big East Tournament quarterfinal.
Bob Falcetti/Icon SMI

Editor's Note

Some team must be the preseason favorite to win a national college basketball championship. The recognition is a joyful thing most of the time, a compliment, an acknowledgment of supposed excellence. But for the University of Connecticut women's basketball team, it was a piano to be lugged. UConn wasn't just the top-ranked team in November 2003, it was the presumptive 2004 champion. The Huskies were national champions the previous year, a smooth-operating, talent-laden, tradition-rich, wonderfully coached unit that moved through opponents and challenges with frightening efficiency. And that team returned intact, led by a player who many believe is the best in the history of the collegiate women's game.

UConn wasn't favored to win; it was expected to win, and nowhere were those expectations stronger than in the state of Connecticut, where a women's title is as certain as runaway real estate taxes and screaming fall foliage. The expectations are a heavy burden every season, and in 2003-04, they were staggering. They took a toll.

Duke showed that Connecticut could be beaten when a last-second shot ended an incredible comeback and brought a victory in a place that rarely provides them—Hartford's Civic Center, filled with the usual 16,294 fans. Three games later, the Huskies were hammered on the road at Notre Dame. Villanova clipped them in the second to last game of the regular season, and Boston College handled the Huskies in the Big East semifinals. UConn could not win its own conference tournament. Connecticut showed it could be beaten in up-tempo games and in deliberately played games. The best players seemed to disappear at important moments. A royally displeased Coach Geno Auriemma publicly sniped at his team, offering particularly harsh assessments of superstar Diana Taurasi.

It is a measure of UConn's talent, heart and resolve that the rest of the postseason was a triumphal march. Greatness was exhibited—in the coaching of Auriemma and the play of his veteran team. Point guard Maria Conlon was unflappable. Barbara Turner emerged as a powerful presence inside and outside. Willnett Crockett was an invaluable contributor from the bench. And Taurasi was everything she was supposed to be, a player never to be forgotten, an individual who probably has elevated her sport in ways that only the greatest of athletes can manage. A fifth straight trip to the Final Four resulted in a third straight national championship and the fifth in 10 years.

The Hartford Courant was with this team throughout the season, bringing hungry readers reports and columns that were deep and insightful and photographs that measured the high moments and the depressions. The work of beat reporter Jeff Goldberg, women's basketball reporter Lori Riley and columnist Jeff Jacobs captured the season in its totality and isolated the key moments, the telling adjustments, the necessary context, and the passions.

Readers of *The Hartford Courant* were wonderfully served by the newspaper's coverage. And that coverage is captured in this book. I know it will allow you to rekindle the memories of 2003-04—a magical season for the storied University of Connecticut women's basketball program.

Brian Toolan

Brian Toolan

Editor

GENO'S LAMENT: STORRS ENVY OF NATION

By Jeff Jacobs *The Hartford Courant*

With the splashy front covers come the slashing back stabs. With the wildly partisan support at Gampel Pavilion come the conspiratorial whispers from pavilions outside of Connecticut.

Is it jealousy? Is it righteousness? Or both? And how does one begin to quantify purity of motive? With the glory comes the gory, and maybe that's only fair with big-time college athletics. If you can make the expectations stand up on the court, make the ethics and principles stand up, too. Run the gauntlet.

UConn isn't the first school under the twin spotlight of adulation and envy, and it won't be the last, but that doesn't make it any less fascinating to watch.

"I'm not sure I want to be here the first week in January when the men's team is No.1, we're No.1, our football team just won a bowl game and everybody wants to know how the hell it happened at that place," Geno Auriemma said. "I can see 75 guys from down in Texas, Oklahoma and Florida going, 'Storrs? Where the hell is that?'

"When you have something and other people are somewhat envious of that, I think they're going to take some shots at you. What you've got to do is hope you don't put yourself in a position where a lot of stuff that people throw at you is true."

There's an edge to the No. 1 story this year, and it doesn't figure to get any less edgy.

Auriemma is so revered in Storrs that one word from him to stop going nuts every time reserve Stacey Marron shoots was obliged with considerate silence. Yet Auriemma also said in *Sports Illustrated* that 90 percent of the coaches in the women's game resent him and 90 percent of the coaches in the men's game are jealous of him.

"One of the issues we have today is people play kissy-face through the media and then stab each other in

OPPOSITE: Jessica Moore drives towards the basket during the UConn women's Super Show in Gampel Pavilion, the start of women's basketball practice.
Tia Ann Chapman/The Hartford Courant

PRESEASON

ABOVE: Willnett Crockett (right), sprained her ankle during Monday's practice and sat on the sidelines with her crutches during Tuesday's practice at Gampel Pavilion. Joining her on the scorer's table following practice are teammates Jessica Moore (left) and Ann Strother (center). *Stephen Dunn/The Hartford Courant*

the back whenever they get a chance," Auriemma said. "I don't want to play any games. I know when you're No. 1 in the country, your friends are the ones who have been your friends all your life, and everybody else wants what you have or resents what you have. For me to pretend it's not like that is bogus."

Auriemma talked the past week about his displeasure with schools that have recruited their fill, then gone to work phoning recruits around the country and spreading horrible rumors to discourage them from signing with rivals.

"Charde Houston has got a press conference scheduled for a [Wednesday] to sign with Connecticut," he said. "On Sunday, her mother gets a phone call from a mysterious source and the press conference is called off. Where did that call come from?"

Houston ended up signing with UConn, but the process has Auriemma angry and perplexed.

"It's become almost like a business venture and I need suppliers," he said. "Guys around the country have set themselves up as distributors. Their job is to deliver players to certain coaches. The NCAA is trying to get rid of these guys, but they don't know what the answer is. Some of them even run their own rankings [that would be Mike Flynn from the Philadelphia area]."

What camps you attend. What apparel you wear. They are decided by the middleman.

"If you have a daughter on an AAU team, should some coaches be excluded from recruiting because the AAU guy doesn't particularly like that school or he has made an agreement with another school? The system works the other way, too. If you're in bed with an AAU guy and he gets a lot of players, you get them all or you get your share."

Auriemma shakes his head. He considers the price of a No. 1 program. How you have to charge $20 a ticket. How he gets paid $875,000 a year and the athletes get paid nothing.

"There's a lot of things to think about, and none if it was [there] 25 years ago when you're sweeping the floor and saying if I can't teach this kid to back up, I'm getting out of coaching," Auriemma said. "Up until now, the women's world hasn't been like that. Is it getting there? Yeah."

FIRST ACT A REAL SHOW

Jessica Moore looks to pass as she is surrounded by Western Michigan's Lori Crisman (left), Ashley Owens (back center) and Carrie Moore (right) in the second half of UConn's 95-46 win. *John Dunn/Icon SMI*

GOOD PASSING MAKES THE DIFFERENCE

By Jeff Goldberg *The Hartford Courant*

Sometimes UConn wins by 50 and it's hard to tell whether the Huskies played well, because the opponent wasn't talented enough to make a definitive evaluation.

No. 1 UConn won by 49, and even the coach from Western Michigan was enough of a realist to know his team was thoroughly overmatched. But the disparity in talent and on the scoreboard was not the barometer of UConn's 95-46 season-opening victory at Gampel Pavilion. The 10,167 on hand knew the Huskies played well, regardless of the competition.

Led by Diana Taurasi, UConn passed the ball beautifully all afternoon and shot even better. The Huskies made 40 of 63 field goal attempts, 63.5 percent, and had 34 assists.

"If you could put a blueprint on how Connecticut plays, today probably would have been it," said Taurasi, who led UConn with 26 points, eight rebounds and seven assists. "Right now, there's a really good feeling on this team that the more you give it up, the more you're going to be rewarded. We have people who want

to be unselfish, and it's coming out now. Our best teams in the past, that's how they've been."

Taurasi made 10 of 11 shots, including five of six three-pointers, and has 1,614 career points, 64 behind sixth-place Shea Ralph on UConn's all-time list.

Taurasi could have taken a run at her career high of 35 points without much difficulty. But she looked instead to get others involved, and the passing was contagious.

"The ball movement was unbelievable today," said Ann Strother, who had 10 points. "I think that's our personality. Everyone's always looking to make the extra pass."

When Ashley Battle converted a baseline layup off a pass from the top of the key by Strother with 6:39 left in the first half, UConn led 38-13 and had assists on all 17 field goals.

Those baskets included four three-pointers by Taurasi, who had 16 points in the first 11 minutes. Taurasi's fourth three-pointer, with 9:16 left in the half,

---

OPPOSITE: Ann Strother drives past Western Michigan's Lori Crisman (left) in the first half at Gampel Pavilion in Storrs, Connecticut. *John Dunn/Icon SMI*

GAME 1 | NOVEMBER 23, 2003

came on sophomore Barbara Turner's fifth assist. Turner, who finished with seven assists, never had more than four in a game last season.

UConn had eight players with at least two assists.

"We've always been a good passing team," UConn coach Geno Auriemma said. "Passing is an art form, and I'm not sure you can make people into great passers that don't already have some of that in them. When your best player is willing to pass the ball as much as Diana does, everyone who thinks they're a good passer wants to become an even better passer, and that's where we are right now."

Jessica Moore had 18 points for UConn, which won its 64th straight home game, five short of Tennessee's NCAA record. Battle had 11 points off the bench.

Maria Jilian led Western Michigan with nine points. The Broncos found themselves at Gampel as part of a deal that led to the November 1 football game between the schools. After 75 seconds Sunday, in which Taurasi hit back-to-back threes, the Broncos felt like they were playing five against 11.

Even with UConn moving the ball all over the court, the Huskies committed just 12 turnovers. UConn forced Western Michigan into 20 turnovers and converted them into 33 points.

"I think you have to be impressed with the way they passed the basketball and the way they moved it to find the right person," Western Michigan coach Ron Stewart said. "Unfortunately, we sometimes left them more open than open, and they found them. They really got after it and they have fun doing it."

				1st	2nd	Total
Western Michigan				21	25	46
UConn				53	42	95

Western Michigan

Player	FGM-A	3PM-A	FTM-A	O-D REB	A	BLK	S	TP
51 L. Crisman	3-10	0-1	0-0	2-5	2	1	0	6
40 K. Koerber	0-1	0-0	0-0	0-0	0	0	0	0
12 M. Jilian	3-10	2-6	1-2	2-1	4	0	2	9
32 C. Rost	2-10	1-8	3-4	1-2	0	0	1	8
33 C. Moore	2-5	2-4	2-4	0-3	1	1	1	8
04 J. Doyle	0-0	0-0	0-0	0-0	0	0	0	0
05 K. Verseput	1-4	1-4	0-0	0-1	1	0	1	3
15 B. Tyson	1-6	0-0	2-4	1-0	4	0	2	4
25 A. Solmose	0-0	0-0	0-0	0-0	0	0	0	0
30 N. Watkins	1-1	1-1	0-0	0-0	0	0	0	3
31 K. Driggett	1-2	1-1	0-0	1-0	0	0	1	3
53 A. Owens	1-2	0-0	0-1	0-1	0	0	0	2
43 M. Jackson	0-0	0-0	0-0	0-0	0	0	0	0

UConn

Player	FGM-A	3PM-A	FTM-A	O-D REB	A	BLK	S	TP
03 D. Taurasi	10-11	5-6	1-1	2-6	7	0	2	26
33 B. Turner	3-6	0-1	0-0	0-1	7	1	0	6
31 J. Moore	9-12	0-0	0-0	1-3	2	0	1	18
05 M. Conlon	2-3	2-3	0-0	0-1	6	0	1	6
43 A. Strother	4-8	1-3	1-1	0-2	3	1	3	10
02 A. Valley	1-3	0-1	3-4	1-3	4	0	2	5
12 S. Marron	1-4	1-3	0-0	1-1	0	0	0	3
20 M. Valley	2-3	0-0	0-0	1-3	2	1	2	4
21 N. Wolff	3-7	0-0	0-0	0-5	1	1	0	6
22 A. Battle	5-6	0-0	1-3	2-1	2	0	3	11

> "The ball movement was unbelievable today."
> —*Ann Strother*

OPPOSITE: Nicole Wolff shoots over Western Michigan's Carrie Moore (33) in the second half. Wolff came off the bench to score six points and grab five rebounds. *John Dunn/Icon SMI*

NOT ABOUT TO BACK OFF

Diana Taurasi and company confer on the court. Four players scored in double figures during a 26-point rout of Arizona State. *John Dunn/Icon SMI*

UCONN NOTCHES 600TH ALL-TIME WIN

By Jeff Goldberg *The Hartford Courant*

Even the top-ranked Huskies can get pushed around. Florida State did it. So did Southern Cal. And for the first 24 minutes against Arizona State, the Sun Devils did a pretty good job, too.

Then the Huskies pushed back. In a flash, the game was over. UConn reached 600 all-time wins with an 81-55 victory at the Civic Center. But it wasn't secure until well into the second half.

Diana Taurasi, who led the Huskies with 22 points despite being visibly frustrated much of the night, was the catalyst. She scored 13 points in a 23-5 stretch, including two three-point baskets and a three-point play.

UConn turned a 43-40 lead with 15:36 left into a 66-45 advantage with 8:57 to play, putting the game away with a 16-0 run.

"I think from here on out we just need to expect that we're going to get hit, and hit, and hit," said Taurasi, who also had seven assists. "You can't let it affect the way you play, even though it's hard when every time you move you have someone hitting you in the chest.

It's something we all have to get accustomed to. These games will help us down the line."

As teams have been doing with regularity this season, Arizona State treated Taurasi like a pinball, knocking her off screens and often leaving her appealing to the officials or looking skyward to a higher power.

So, too, were the Huskies after a first half in which they shot 51.7 percent and outrebounded Arizona State 21-16, yet led by only 34-32 because of 10 turnovers that the Sun Devils turned into 13 points. Taurasi vented some of her frustrations in the locker room at halftime.

"One thing about this team that I respect is if you have something to say, everyone is big enough to take it," Taurasi said. "Effort-wise, I thought we were there, but applying it and getting stuff done, we weren't doing it. That's when you have to take it possession by possession."

With UConn leading 43-40, Taurasi scored on a post-up play. After she hit two free throws to make it 47-42,

OPPOSITE: Diana Taurasi gets off to a good start, scoring the first two points of the game on this drive. Taurasi led the Huskies with 22 points. *Stephen Dunn/The Hartford Courant*

ABOVE: Barbara Turner and Arizona State's Amy Denson struggle for control of the ball in the second half in Hartford.
Stephen Dunn/The Hartford Courant

Taurasi was called for her third foul with 13:32 left and complained bitterly to referee Connie Pardue.

But when UConn got the ball back, Ashley Battle found Taurasi in the corner for a three-pointer that gave the Huskies a 50-42 lead, their biggest of the night.

After an Arizona State three-point play, UConn ripped off 16 straight, starting with a five-point play. As Taurasi was making another three-pointer from the top of the key, Battle was fouled under the basket. And with the Sun Devils already in the penalty, Battle made both free throws for a 55-45 lead with 12:15 left.

"We knew that a lot of teams come in here and hang around for a half and get blown out," Arizona State coach Charli Turner Thorne said. "We knew they would go to Diana. We knew they'd get more aggressive on defense. We just didn't stop it."

Taurasi's driving three-point play and five straight points by Ann Strother gave UConn the 66-45 lead with 8:57 left.

"In the first half, it probably looked like they were more physical than us," said Barbara Turner, who had nine points. "In the second half, we did a good job of coming out and hitting them back and being really aggressive."

	1st	2nd	Total
Arizona State	32	23	55
UConn	34	47	81

Arizona State

Player	FGM-A	3PM-A	FTM-A	O-D REB	A	BLK	S	TP
33 A. Denson	3-6	1-1	2-4	0-1	1	0	1	9
54 K. Kovesdy	4-8	0-1	5-6	1-4	0	1	0	13
10 K. Loney	4-12	3-7	0-0	1-2	3	0	0	11
23 B. Boardman	1-7	1-5	0-0	1-1	1	0	2	3
30 C. Buckner	2-4	0-0	1-2	1-0	2	0	2	5
34 Y. Rosenthal	1-5	1-2	0-0	2-0	1	0	0	3
04 E. Westerberg	1-5	0-2	0-0	1-0	0	0	1	2
05 L. Stagg	0-0	0-0	0-0	0-0	0	0	0	0
12 A. Godette	1-6	1-1	0-0	2-0	0	0	0	3
31 J. Albert	0-0	0-0	2-2	0-0	0	0	0	2
32 A. Johnson	0-1	0-0	0-0	0-0	0	0	0	0
44 J. Thigpin	2-3	0-0	0-0	1-4	2	1	0	4

UConn

Player	FGM-A	3PM-A	FTM-A	O-D REB	A	BLK	S	TP
33 B. Turner	4-12	0-0	1-4	4-1	1	0	0	9
43 A. Strother	4-6	2-3	2-5	2-4	2	0	2	12
31 J. Moore	6-8	0-0	3-5	1-6	2	1	0	15
03 D. Taurasi	8-14	2-3	4-4	1-2	7	2	3	22
05 M. Conlon	2-4	2-4	0-0	0-3	1	0	0	6
02 A. Valley	1-1	0-0	1-2	0-1	1	0	1	3
04 K. Robinson	1-2	0-0	0-0	0-1	0	0	0	2
12 S. Marron	0-0	0-0	0-0	0-0	0	0	0	0
20 M. Valley	0-0	0-0	0-0	1-1	1	1	0	0
22 A. Battle	4-4	0-0	2-4	2-5	2	1	2	10
34 L. Sherwood	1-2	0-0	0-0	0-0	0	3	0	2

UConn (600-261) is the 24th women's program with at least 600 victories. On December 5, 1974, UConn beat Eastern Connecticut 40-27 for win No. 1.

"We knew they would go to Diana... We just didn't stop it."
—Charli Turner Thorne, Arizona State

BARBARA TURNER #33

By Jeff Goldberg *The Hartford Courant*

Barbara Turner averaged 10.2 assists as a high school senior. That's four more a game than Diana Taurasi averaged her senior season, three more than Maria Conlon.

Yet the party line in the UConn locker room heading into this season was that the next pass Turner made in a game would be her first. She had just 45 assists last season. "When she was an incoming freshman the coaches were always talking about, 'Barbara's a really good passer,'" Taurasi said after UConn's 95-46 victory over Western Michigan. "And last year, I was like, she doesn't pass. How is she a really good passer?"

Turner said the biggest difference this season is her comfort level. As a freshman, Turner struggled to learn the offense. By the end of the year, she had become one of UConn's top scoring options, setting up in the lane and scoring on post-ups. Now, she has a better read on what the defense is throwing at her.

"That's something I've always had," Turner said. "Coming out of high school I was always a passer. It was just a matter last year where I just wasn't comfortable in our offense. I just didn't know how to get into the right spots. This year, I'm a lot more comfortable.

"I'm not as tentative as I was last year—should I make the pass, should I shoot? If I get the ball on the block, I'm going to look to score, but if I'm being double-teamed, then I'm going to look for the open man. That's something you look to do when you come to Connecticut. We don't have one person that wants to take every shot. That's what makes us effective."

Taurasi has often said it takes a full year for a player to settle into a comfort zone, and she can see it happening with Turner.

"The game's slowed down for her now," Taurasi said. "When you can score at will like she can—every time she touches the ball, she can score on anyone in the country—she's going to draw a lot of attention. For her now to kick it and get people open, that makes her that much better. If she doesn't get the assist, she'll make the pass that leads to the assist, which is just as good."

Turner said the way she's being used at UConn is similar to the way she played at East Tech High School in Cleveland, where she averaged a triple-double as a senior. Her versatile game, passing included, is what attracted the UConn coaching staff to her.

"Barbara's on her way to becoming a pretty good basketball player," Auriemma said. "I don't know what I'm going to have to complain about after that. She's made a lot of progress, that kid. The few times that I really concentrate on watching her play, she has great instincts, and the more she works at it, the better she's getting. But you didn't have to be Oscar Robertson to find the open man [in the opener]."

All the Huskies passed well, as the team racked up 34 assists on 40 field goals. But it was the "7" next to Turner's name on the stat sheet that made the biggest impression in the locker room.

"She's passing the ball really well," Ann Strother said. "I think last year there was a little bit of, 'Barbara can't pass.' And she wants to prove people wrong, because she's a great passer."

Name: Barbara Turner
Born: June 8, 1984
Hometown: Cleveland, Ohio
High School: East Technical High
School
Position: Forward
Height: 6'0"
Major: Undecided
Class: Sophomore

HOME COOKING

OPPOSITE: Ashley Valley steals the ball from Keisha Brown during the game against North Carolina State at the Hartford Civic Center. UConn defeated NC State 87-53. *(Bob MacDonnell/The Hartford Courant)*

HUSKIES LOOK ALMOST PERFECT

By Jeff Goldberg *The Hartford Courant*

It took two games over eight days, but UConn finally put together the closest thing to a perfect 40 minutes.

The top-ranked Huskies, brilliant in the second half against St. Joseph's on Dec. 21, kept the good times rolling against North Carolina State, building a 23-point, first-half lead in an 87-53 victory before 16,294 at the Civic Center. UConn won its 69th consecutive home game, tying Tennessee (1990-96) for the longest such streak in Division I history.

UConn made 12 of its first 14 shots against the Wolfpack and did not commit a turnover until 7:32 remained in the first half. By then, the Huskies led 30-12.

"I think the first eight games we were trying to find ourselves," said Diana Taurasi, who had 18 points and a season-high eight assists. "But I think the St. Joe's game and this game, we kind of got the sense that when we got on the court, we were going to dominate."

Ann Strother got the Huskies going Monday, scoring UConn's first eight points. The sophomore guard finished with a career-high 20.

"I think I need to come out like that a lot more often," said Strother, who had a career-high five three-pointers. "I felt like I needed to be a lot more aggressive at the start of the game. We all do. It's something we've been lacking."

Strother hit two threes in the opening burst and had two more in a 23-5 run in the second half.

Eight players scored for UConn in the first half, in which Strother and Barbara Turner (17 points) reached double figures.

"We wanted to build on what happened last weekend," UConn coach Geno Auriemma said. "You're only as good as your next game. Tonight was the next game. It's still early. I don't know that we're completely there. It's an ongoing process. You want to see progress, and there has been."

UConn's frontcourt got an unexpected boost when sophomore forward Willnett Crockett checked in with

OPPOSITE: Ann Strother hits one of her five three pointers over Keisha Brown. Strother led the team with 20 points. *Bob MacDonnell/The Hartford Courant*

6:42 remaining. Crockett missed the first eight games with a severe right ankle sprain and was not expected to play. She scored one point on a free throw with 3:05 left and had one rebound.

NC State center Kaayla Chones, who entered the game averaging 14.2 points and 7.5 rebounds, was a non-factor with 15 points—four in the first half—and five rebounds. Kendra Bell had 11 points for the Wolfpack.

Strother's back-to-back three-pointers gave UConn an 8-2 lead.

The Huskies extended their lead to 16-7 with 14:04 left in the half; then Taurasi got hot. She made a jumper and a layup 57 seconds apart. She hit Jessica Moore with a no-look pass for a layup, made a step-back jumper with two seconds on the shot clock and floated home a tear-dropper in the lane.

Strother capped an 11-0 run by faking a pick-and-roll with Turner and driving to the basket for a three-point play. With 11:10 remaining in the half, UConn had a 27-9 lead.

UConn finished the half making 20 of 34 shots and committing three turnovers, while holding NC State to nine-for-30 shooting.

Moore's slump continued as she became the first UConn player to foul out this season, and she did it in just 13 minutes, scoring four points and grabbing five rebounds. Moore picked up her fifth foul with 14:06 left.

	1st	2nd	Total
NC State	24	29	53
UConn	47	40	87

NC State

Player	FGM-A	3PM-A	FTM-A	O-D REB	A	BLK	S	TP
34 A. Mendeng	3-8	0-0	0-0	3-0	0	1	0	6
50 K. Chones	6-17	0-0	3-5	1-4	0	0	0	15
03 K. Brown	2-6	0-1	3-4	1-3	0	0	1	7
14 N. Rivers	2-4	0-0	0-0	0-0	2	0	1	4
30 K. Bell	2-5	1-1	6-7	0-2	2	0	1	11
01 T. James	0-2	0-0	1-2	0-1	0	0	1	1
02 R. Stockdale	0-2	0-1	2-2	1-2	0	0	0	2
04 S. Reaves	0-0	0-0	0-0	0-1	1	0	0	0
10 L. Bailey	1-3	1-3	0-0	1-0	1	0	0	3
11 M. Pope	0-0	0-0	0-0	0-0	0	0	1	0
12 M. Dickens	0-0	0-0	0-0	0-0	0	1	0	0
13 B. McDowell	0-3	0-1	0-0	1-1	1	0	0	0
15 A. Key	1-1	0-0	0-0	0-0	0	0	0	2
25 K. Gissendanner	1-2	0-1	0-0	0-0	0	0	1	2

UConn

Player	FGM-A	3PM-A	FTM-A	O-D REB	A	BLK	S	TP
33 B. Turner	8-10	0-1	1-1	2-1	4	0	1	17
43 A. Strother	7-12	5-8	1-1	0-2	2	0	1	20
31 J. Moore	2-4	0-0	0-0	0-5	1	1	0	4
03 D. Taurasi	8-13	1-5	1-1	0-1	8	0	2	18
05 M. Conlon	2-3	1-2	0-0	1-3	4	0	0	5
02 A. Valley	1-3	0-2	2-4	2-1	2	0	2	4
04 K. Robinson	1-4	1-2	0-0	1-2	0	0	0	3
12 S. Marron	0-0	0-0	0-0	0-0	0	0	0	0
20 M. Valley	1-5	0-0	2-2	2-1	0	1	2	4
22 A. Battle	2-5	0-1	0-0	2-3	1	0	1	4
23 W. Crockett	0-0	0-0	1-2	1-0	0	0	0	1
34 L. Sherwood	2-5	0-0	3-6	1-2	2	2	1	7

OPPOSITE: Ashley Battle drives for a layup over Rachel Stockdale. Battle scored four of the bench's 23 points in the 34-point victory. *Bob MacDonnell/The Hartford Courant*

"You're only as good as your next game."

—*Geno Auriemma*

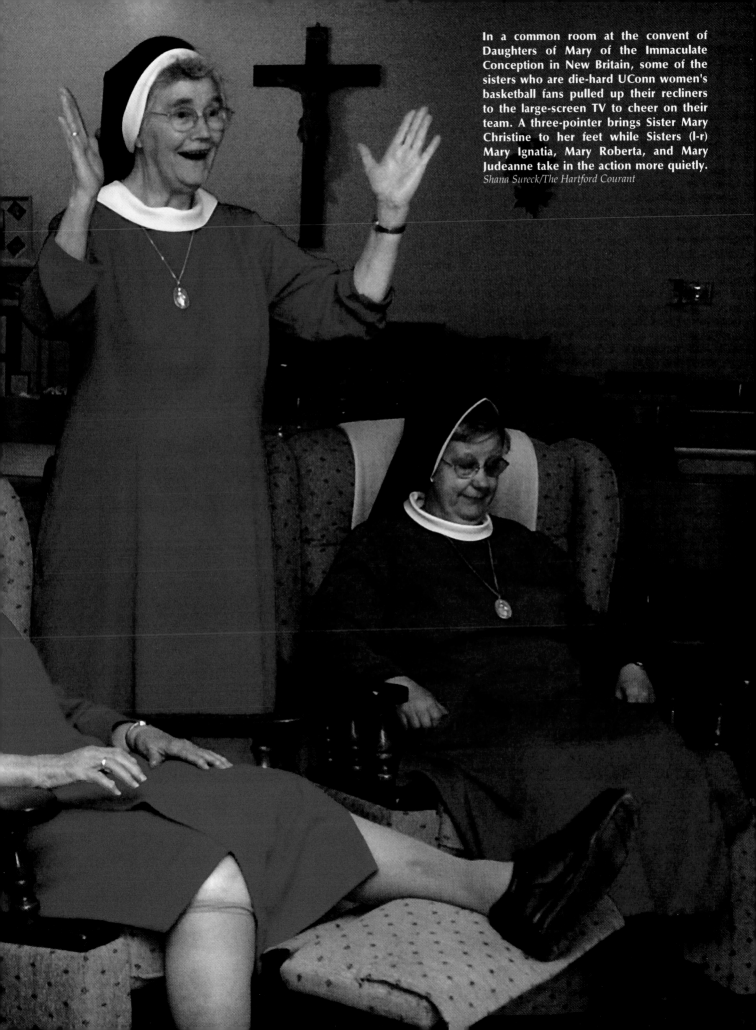

In a common room at the convent of Daughters of Mary of the Immaculate Conception in New Britain, some of the sisters who are die-hard UConn women's basketball fans pulled up their recliners to the large-screen TV to cheer on their team. A three-pointer brings Sister Mary Christine to her feet while Sisters (l-r) Mary Ignatia, Mary Roberta, and Mary Judeanne take in the action more quietly.
Shana Sureck/The Hartford Courant

WORN SILVER

Ann Strother (center) and the rest of the UConn women's basketball team stand stunned after losing to Duke by one point at the buzzer at the Hartford Civic Center. Coach Geno Auriemma and associate head coach Chris Dailey are at right. *Cloe Poisson/The Hartford Courant*

Duke 68 | **UConn 67**

UCONN LOSES AT BUZZER IN NEW UNIFORMS

By Jeff Goldberg *The Hartford Courant*

UConn coach Geno Auriemma was asked about his team's decade of dominance at home. UConn's approach was simple, Auriemma said. The Huskies don't lose home games. They might get beat, but they never give away games.

At the Civic Center against Duke, UConn gave a big one away. The top-ranked Huskies seemed on the verge of completing a carbon copy of last year's blowout victory over Duke, leading the No. 4 Blue Devils by 20 in the first half and by 14 with 3:53 to play.

Then, suddenly, it all came undone. Energized by a full-court trap that paralyzed UConn in the final minutes, Duke came all the way back, stunning the Huskies—and a boisterous crowd of 16,294—on Jessica Foley's three-pointer at the buzzer for a 68-67 victory.

The loss marked the first time in Auriemma's 19-year tenure that UConn lost after leading by 20 and ended their record-tying, 69-game home winning streak. The team came in wearing the new silver uniforms the coach brought out for the occasion.

"That worked out good, didn't it?" Auriemma said.

The Huskies, who dominated the first 30 minutes, committed six turnovers in the final 2:02 as Duke's press worked to perfection. UConn got the ball over halfcourt twice in its final eight possessions as Duke ended the game on a 14-2 run.

Diana Taurasi led UConn with 16 points, but shot only five for 16 and had five turnovers. Barbara Turner, who also had five turnovers, had 15 points and eight rebounds. Jessica Moore had 14 points and eight rebounds.

Alana Beard scored 20 of her 21 points in the second half for Duke. Monique Currie had 17 points and seven rebounds.

The 69-game streak leaves the Huskies tied with Tennessee for the NCAA record. The Huskies hadn't

OPPOSITE: Diana Taurasi scores to give UConn a two-point lead with five seconds left, but it wasn't enough. Duke's Jessica Foley made a three at the buzzer to win the game. *Michael McAndrews/The Hartford Courant*

lost a home game since February 2, 2000—a one-point loss to Tennessee that ended on a UConn miss at the buzzer.

It appeared UConn had No. 70 in a row sewn up at halftime. Last year, UConn took a 21-point halftime lead at Cameron Indoor Stadium and eventually led by 28 before Duke closed to six in the final minute.

This time, UConn led 35-15 with 1:11 left in the half.

"When it got to be a 20-point lead for them, it became deja vu all over again, like last year," Duke coach Gail Goestenkors said. "I was just proud of the team. They showed a great deal of maturity. Last year they were happy just to make a comeback; this year that wasn't going to be enough."

Duke cut the lead to nine with 5:24 left, but UConn scored five straight, and when Taurasi made one of two free throws with 2:37 left, UConn led, 65-54.

But Beard started the Blue Devils on their final, frantic run. She stole the ball from Turner and hit a jumper with 1:56 left.

"They started pressing, and we really didn't have an answer for it," Taurasi said. "We worked on it in practice and we thought we had a handle on it. It just didn't work out."

"I think we lost our energy at the end of the game," said Auriemma, who used six players most of the way. "Mentally, we broke down. The look on their faces when they'd come over to the bench, I didn't know what to tell them. Each timeout, it got worse and worse."

But UConn almost escaped with the victory, getting the ball back with 20 seconds left and going to Taurasi,

OPPOSITE: Duke's Alana Beard ties the game 65-65 with a layup over Barbara Turner with 40 seconds left. The lead would change twice more in the last minute. *Cloe Poisson/The Hartford Courant*

	1st	2nd	Total
Duke	18	50	68
UConn	35	32	67

Duke

Player	FGM-A	3PM-A	FTM-A	O-D REB	A	BLK	S	TP
25 M. Currie	6-13	2-4	3-5	4-3	1	0	0	17
33 I. Tillis	3-15	0-4	0-0	3-7	4	0	2	6
01 M. Bass	2-4	0-0	2-3	3-1	0	1	0	6
10 L. Harding	3-9	2-3	0-0	0-2	3	0	2	8
20 A. Beard	9-24	1-5	2-4	4-2	1	4	5	21
12 V. Krapohl	0-0	0-0	0-0	0-0	0	0	0	0
24 J. Foley	3-6	2-4	0-0	0-3	1	0	1	8
43 A. Bales	0-0	0-0	0-0	0-0	0	0	0	0
44 B. Hunter	1-4	0-0	0-0	0-6	1	1	2	2

UConn

Player	FGM-A	3PM-A	FTM-A	O-D REB	A	BLK	S	TP
33 B. Turner	5-12	0-2	5-8	4-4	3	0	0	15
43 A. Strother	3-5	2-3	4-4	0-5	3	2	1	12
31 J. Moore	6-8	0-0	2-9	0-8	2	2	0	14
03 D. Taurasi	5-16	3-8	3-4	1-3	3	2	0	16
05 M. Conlon	1-6	1-5	0-0	0-4	4	0	0	3
20 M. Valley	0-0	0-0	0-0	0-0	1	0	0	0
22 A. Battle	3-7	0-0	1-2	4-5	2	0	2	7
23 W. Crockett	0-0	0-0	0-0	0-1	0	0	0	0

who dropped in a leaner over Beard with 4.6 seconds left for a 67-65 lead.

With no timeouts, Duke's Lindsey Harding rushed the ball upcourt and found Foley on the right wing. Ann Strother rushed and leaped at Foley, but not before Foley released the ball with eight-tenths of a second left. It swished through, and the entire Duke team rushed across the court and piled on the sophomore guard from Australia.

"I felt like I was wide open, and then as soon as I got the ball, there was Ann Strother coming straight at my face," said Foley, who was recruited by UConn. "I just got it up there somehow."

"I was pretty close," Strother said. "But not close enough."

JESSICA MOORE #31

By Jeff Goldberg *The Hartford Courant*

For two years, Jessica Moore studied the art of post defense under the master. Asjha Jones was as tough and reliable a defensive center as UConn has ever had. Some of the top post players in the nation took their shot at Jones two seasons ago. All were turned away as UConn went undefeated.

Now, the hub of UConn's defense is Moore. The six-foot-three junior is quicker, more lithe than the powerful Jones, but the results have essentially been the same. In recent games, Moore has neutralized some the best post players in the Atlantic Coast Conference. North Carolina State's Kaayla Chones was a non-factor in the first as UConn took a big lead. Mistie Bass and Brittany Hunter had little to do with Duke's comeback, and Moore had 14 points and eight rebounds.

"I try to get into my game by setting the tone on defense and letting the offense come to me," said Moore, who is averaging 10.6 points and 6.5 rebounds. "But I really get my confidence through my defense, so I like to think their problems come from me."

"The bigger the challenge," UConn coach Geno Auriemma said, "the better Jessica usually performs."

Auriemma says Moore is close to earning the accolades that Georgetown's Rebekkah Brunson receives. Brunson was a first-team All-Big East selection last season and a preseason first-teamer this year, but Moore is not using today's matchup as a personal platform.

"I just think about, this is their best player and I'm going to play her like any other really good player," Moore said. "Try to take her out of her game. She's very patient and she uses her body very well. If you take away one thing, she's going to try and get it another

way. She doesn't give up so easy. If anything, I'm going to try to learn a little bit from her."

From being Jones's understudy, Moore learned to use positioning as a defensive weapon, bumping and angling opponents away from their favorite spots on the blocks. That might be more difficult against Brunson, who is comfortable on the perimeter as well as down low.

"I don't think Jessica can change what she does," Auriemma said. "She's not all of a sudden going to be more physical than Brunson. It's just going to be keeping her away from her comfort zone. Not letting Brunson go where she wants to go. You have to keep her off the backboard when the other guys shoot. It's one thing when she has the ball. She's pretty dangerous when the other guys shoot, too."

"I'm keeping up my confidence level," Moore said. "Now that we're getting into Big East play, it's time to bear down and start playing well."

Next, Moore will face Notre Dame's talented front line. Then there is Rutgers and six-foot-three Shalicia Hurns and Virginia Tech's six-foot-four Ieva Kublina.

"She's got a lot of good matchups coming up," Auriemma said. "Jessica always does a good job. Generally speaking, except when she's gotten a couple of fouls early, Jessica is pretty reliable.

"She's one of the few kids in our locker room that does put up some goals that she wants to accomplish. She's very goal-oriented. She'll say to herself, this is what I want to do today, and generally she'll do it. Once she decides she's going to do it, it gets done. That's why I love her."

40

Name: Jessica Moore
Born: July 9,1982
Hometown: Palmer, Arkansas
High School: Colony High School
Position: Center
Height: 6'3"
Major: Communications
Class: Junior

TALKING POINT

Maria Conlon tries to hold on to a loose ball under UConn's basket. Georgetown forward Varda Tamoulianis pressures her. *Michael McAndrews/The Hartford Courant*

UConn 69 | **Georgetown 51**

LEAVE IT TO DIANA

By Jeff Goldberg *The Hartford Courant*

It started two minutes into the game. Diana Taurasi took a shot that rattled halfway in the basket. Jessica Moore, in perfect rebounding position, saw the ball going through and turned to run back on defense.

But the Gampel Pavilion rim, usually friendly to the home team, spit the ball out, exactly to the spot Moore had just occupied. Georgetown got the rebound. It was the first indication it would be an unusual afternoon. Fourth-ranked UConn beat the Hoyas 69-51 before 10,167, but how the Huskies got there, and what happened afterward, was anything but routine.

UConn missed 12 straight shots, starting with Taurasi's rattler, and had its lowest-scoring first half of the season, trailing 29-26. It was the first time in four years the Huskies trailed a Big East opponent at halftime at home.

Taurasi led the Huskies with 21 points, but she missed nine of her first 10 shots and needed a career-high 23 attempts to make seven. Taurasi was three for 12 from three, and her day mirrored the team's effort in the first half as shot after shot danced tantalizingly on the rim before bouncing out.

After scoring the first five points, UConn went nine minutes without a field goal, trailing 10-5 with 11:53 left in the half.

"There's a lot of things that have happened to this team in the last two weeks that you can't explain," Taurasi said.

That included an interview ban imposed by coach Geno Auriemma after the game. A day after Auriemma said he wanted to give Taurasi a breather from media-related duties, she was the only player he allowed to talk after the game as a form of punishment for the rest of the team.

After weeks of hearing and reading that his players say they need to give Taurasi more help, Auriemma instituted a rare gag order.

"There's a time for talking, and there's a time for playing," Auriemma said. "If you want to become a celebrity and get interviewed by the media, you ought to do something to earn it."

OPPOSITE: Diana Taurasi and Jessica Moore trap Georgetown forward Rebekkah Brunson in the second half. UConn went on to win 69-51. *Michael McAndrews/The Hartford Courant*

But just as quickly as he buried his players, Auriemma praised them for riding out the wayward shooting in the first half.

UConn recovered, as it usually does, by hitting Georgetown with a 21-3 run to start the second half. The Huskies took Hoyas center Rebekkah Brunson out of the game from the start, holding the All-America candidate to eight points and seven rebounds, well below her season averages.

"Actually, we didn't play badly. We just shot horribly," Auriemma said. "But when you shoot well, everyone thinks you played well, and when you shoot badly, everyone thinks you played badly."

Sophomore guard Ann Strother shot poorly (two for nine) and played well, with eight points, nine rebounds, eight assists and three blocks. Senior guard Maria Conlon, who had been shooting poorly, made three of five three-pointers and had 12 points. Freshman Liz Sherwood shot and played well, with a career-high 11 points.

As in its previous game at Gampel December 2 against Siena, UConn trailed the vast majority of the first half. But Georgetown could not capitalize.

After taking a 10-5 lead four minutes into game, Georgetown had seven turnovers in the next 6:15 and didn't score until UConn had closed to 10-9 with 9:40 left.

"It was on offense and execution, and putting the ball in the basket was our downfall," Georgetown coach Pat Knapp said. "We have to score points. [UConn] played hard, but some of the mistakes were self-inflicted."

OPPOSITE: Diana Taurasi drives between Georgetown guard Carmen Bruce and forward Varda Tamoulianis in the second half. Taurasi finished with a game-high 21 points in the 69-51 win at Gampel Pavillion in Storrs.
Michael McAndrews/The Hartford Courant

	1st	2nd	Total
Georgetown	29	22	51
UConn	26	43	69

Georgetown

Player	FGM-A	3PM-A	FTM-A	O-D REB	A	BLK	S	TP
32 R. Brunson	3-11	0-0	2-4	1-6	3	0	0	8
44 V. Tamoulianis	5-8	0-0	3-7	1-6	2	1	1	13
05 M. Lisicky	3-10	3-5	0-0	1-2	2	0	0	9
24 B. Lesueur	0-4	0-0	2-5	3-3	1	0	0	2
25 C. Bruce	1-8	0-0	1-2	2-2	3	0	2	3
03 K. Carlin	4-8	1-1	2-2	2-0	0	0	0	11
10 N. Berggren	1-1	0-0	0-0	0-0	0	0	0	2
12 L. Tyburski	0-0	0-0	1-2	0-1	0	0	0	1
22 S. Jenkins	1-3	0-1	0-0	0-0	1	0	0	2

UConn

Player	FGM-A	3PM-A	FTM-A	O-D REB	A	BLK	S	TP
33 B. Turner	2-5	0-0	2-2	0-3	3	0	1	6
43 A. Strother	2-9	2-8	2-2	3-6	8	3	0	8
31 J. Moore	1-5	0-0	3-4	2-5	1	0	1	5
03 D. Taurasi	7-23	3-12	4-5	4-3	3	3	0	21
05 M. Conlon	4-7	3-5	1-2	1-1	2	0	2	12
02 A. Valley	0-1	0-0	0-0	1-0	0	0	0	0
12 S. Marron	0-1	0-1	0-0	0-0	0	0	0	0
20 M. Valley	1-2	0-0	1-2	1-2	0	0	2	3
22 A. Battle	0-1	0-0	1-2	0-2	1	0	1	1
23 W. Crockett	1-1	0-0	0-0	1-1	0	4	0	2
34 L. Sherwood	5-6	0-0	1-1	0-0	1	0	0	11

UConn scored the first seven points of the second half to take a 33-29 lead with 16:27 left. After a Georgetown free throw, Taurasi hit back-to-back threes to make it 39-30. Strother hit her second three of the half to put UConn up 10, then Conlon hit a three with 10:42 left to complete the 21-3 run that gave UConn a 47-32 lead.

UConn made three of 14 three-pointers in the first half, but hit five of nine to start the second.

"You can stop shooting them, which means you're not going to miss them, but you're not going to make them," Taurasi said. "I think we've got guys that when you go 0 for five, they're going to take those next five shots. In the second half, we knocked them in, and it opened the game up."

HUSKIES MAKE THEIR STAND

OPPOSITE: Diana Taurasi breaks away from the pack with a second-half steal against Boston College at the Hartford Civic Center. Taurasi failed to convert on her layup. UConn defeated BC 69-61. *Patrick Raycraft/The Hartford Courant*

HUSKIES FIND REDEMPTION

By Jeff Goldberg *The Hartford Courant*

The moment of truth for UConn came with exactly five minutes left. Just as they were last week at Notre Dame, the fourth-ranked Huskies were locked in a tense affair with No. 22 Boston College at the Civic Center, only now they were the ones clinging to a slender lead.

When BC's Clare Droesch made a steal and hit Amber Jacobs downcourt for a layup, UConn's lead was down to three, and coach Geno Auriemma called time out. How the Huskies closed this game would tell a lot about their psyche after two losses in the past four games. "It was the same situation that we've been in," Diana Taurasi said. "Are you going to fight your way out of a corner, or just lay down and take a punch to the face?"

In South Bend, the Huskies took a knockout blow. This time, they were the ones left standing.

Ann Strother scored three times to keep UConn's lead at five, and Ashley Battle rebounded two three-point attempts in the final minute to preserve a 69-61 victory at the Civic Center.

For one afternoon, UConn (12-2, 3-1 Big East) rediscovered the moxie that carried it to a national championship last season.

"When you go through a stretch where you get really good players missing wide-open layups, the ball bounces the wrong way, a 50-50 call goes the wrong way, it's good that you see good stuff happening down the stretch," Auriemma said. "They probably really needed that right now."

It was a day of redemption for several Huskies who struggled during UConn's two-week tailspin. Barbara Turner, who held herself responsible for the Duke loss that started UConn's slide, scored 19 points and made all 11 of her free throws.

Willnett Crockett, who had not contributed in either of UConn's losses, played a season-high 20 minutes and

OPPOSITE: Boston College guard Sarah Marshall tries to drive around Ashley Battle. The win over the Eagles raised the Huskies' league mark to 3-1 and season record to 12-2.
Patrick Raycraft/The Hartford Courant

GAME 14 | JANUARY 17, 2004

UConn 69 | Boston College 61

provided solid defense against the Eagles' formidable front line.

And there was Strother, who did to Boston College what Notre Dame's Jacqueline Batteast did to UConn last week—make key shots to stop a comeback in its tracks.

Strother entered Saturday's game having made seven of her past 25 shots. But after Auriemma's 30-second timeout, she hit a jumper from the free throw line with 4:43 left to put UConn ahead, 59-54. Then she swooped in to put back a Jessica Moore miss with 4:00 left to make it 61-56.

And after Jessalyn Deveny (20 points) hit a three-pointer with 2:09 left to cut UConn's lead to two, Strother got open in the left corner for a three-pointer that danced on the rim before falling in with 1:37 left to make it 64-59.

"I think it hit every part of the rim," said Strother, who had 12 points on five for 10 shooting and five rebounds. "But it went down, so it feels good. Every little thing added a little bit of confidence. It feels like we're starting to get our confidence back."

With UConn leading 65-59 in the final minute, Brooke Queenan twice attempted three-pointers for Boston College but missed both. Battle (eight points, seven rebounds) was there each time and made two free throws after the second with 38.3 seconds left to put UConn up by eight.

UConn, which had scored 26 points in the first half of its previous two games, again struggled and led 27-24 at

---

OPPOSITE: Barbara Turner drives past BC forward Nicole Warren during second-half action. Turner led the Huskies with 19 points. *Patrick Raycraft/The Hartford Courant*

	1st	2nd	Total
Boston College	24	37	61
UConn	27	42	69

Boston College

Player	FGM-A	3PM-A	FTM-A	O-D REB	A	BLK	S	TP
20 A. Parham	2-4	0-1	1-1	0-1	1	0	2	5
55 L. Macchia	1-4	0-0	2-2	2-0	0	0	0	4
25 M. Leahy	1-2	0-0	0-2	1-1	0	2	0	2
00 J. Deveny	6-12	3-5	5-5	2-4	2	0	1	20
23 A. Jacobs	1-7	0-3	2-2	0-4	3	0	0	4
02 B. Queenan	0-4	0-2	0-0	0-2	1	0	0	0
03 S. Marshall	1-2	1-1	0-0	0-0	0	0	0	3
11 K. Ress	5-11	0-0	3-4	1-4	2	1	0	13
15 C. Droesch	3-6	2-2	2-2	2-3	3	0	1	10
21 N. Warren	0-0	0-0	0-0	0-0	0	0	0	0

UConn

Player	FGM-A	3PM-A	FTM-A	O-D REB	A	BLK	S	TP
33 B. Turner	4-7	0-1	11-11	3-2	4	1	1	19
43 A. Strother	5-10	2-3	0-0	2-3	2	0	0	12
31 J. Moore	6-10	0-0	0-1	2-7	0	0	1	12
03 D. Taurasi	4-13	2-4	2-2	0-3	4	1	3	12
05 M. Conlon	1-6	1-5	0-0	0-1	2	0	1	3
22 A. Battle	2-6	0-0	4-5	2-5	1	0	0	8
23 W. Crockett	0-0	0-0	3-4	1-1	0	0	2	3
34 L. Sherwood	0-0	0-0	0-0	0-0	0	0	0	0

the break. UConn could not maintain an early nine-point lead.

Led by Deveny and six-foot-four freshman Kathrin Ress of Italy (13 points), Boston College took a 42-39 lead with 14:00 left. But Turner made four straight free throws to give UConn the lead, and Taurasi hit a three with 11:45 left to put UConn ahead for good at 46-45.

But not until the final minutes did UConn secure the victory—and its peace of mind.

"The last five minutes—deflections, rebounds, hitting free throws—was what we did last year," said Taurasi, who scored 12 points but remains in a shooting slump, going four for 13 including a missed breakaway layup. "Little by little, we're improving. Today, we did a great job of staying in there. On a scale from one to 10, we played a six. But we grinded it out and worked hard."

GENO AURIEMMA

By Jeff Goldberg *The Hartford Courant*

Long before they were reunited on the UConn bench, coach Geno Auriemma and director of basketball operations Jack Eisenmann were basketball brothers in Norristown, Pennsylvania. Under the guidance of a local priest, the teenaged Auriemma and Eisenmann would head for nearby Philadelphia, looking for a game.

"Father Jerry used to pile us in a car to play basketball," Auriemma said. "And sometimes the parents would say, 'Aren't you worried about going into some tough neighborhoods?' He's like, 'I've got a collar on. No one's going to bother us.' Well, that wasn't always true. But you learned to play and not back down from anybody. We weren't going to scare anybody on the court. We didn't have any Kobe Bryants. But we loved to compete. We loved to play. We just wanted a game."

Auriemma has never grown tired of the game, or the competition. His love for basketball and his exposure to the great hoops minds of Philly sent him on a coaching journey that landed him in Storrs 18 years ago, and he hasn't looked back.

In the past 10 seasons, UConn is 339-21. This year's team can become the first in women's basketball history to reach five straight Final Fours and the second to win three straight championships. But even if it doesn't happen, Auriemma is already on the fast track to the Basketball Hall of Fame.

"I think at that time, the hope or the goal was really to become a high school teacher and a high school coach," said St. Joseph's men's coach Phil Martelli, who hired a 24-year-old Auriemma to coach at his alma mater, Bishop Kenrick High School, in 1978. "Never in anyone's wildest imaginations did you think he was going to do this for a living and go down as one of the all-timers, which is what's going to happen. What he's done is astounding."

As Auriemma matured from a high school player under Buddy Gardler at Kenrick in the early 1970s to an assistant's position at Virginia in the early 1980s, he soaked up bits of coaching philosophy from all over the city.

But when fellow coaches and former players speak of Auriemma's greatest strength, it is rarely about Xs and Os.

"We still talk twice a week, and I really think that what he's done ... he has a great sense of joy that they've reached this point," Martelli said. "But he's driven to make it better. Not just maintain, but do it a little better, whether it's practice preparation or scouting reports, or whatever.

"Some people don't take the time to enjoy it. I give him credit. He certainly enjoys and understands what they've done. He's not going to be one of those obsessive guys, but he enjoys exploring the fact that they can do more. He certainly enjoyed last season and that team. And he loved that Sue Bird group. He took time to enjoy that moment last year, because they have the trophy, but they might not have been the best team in the country."

"Nothing lasts forever," Auriemma said. "For us, we know its not going to last forever. How can it? Can you keep it going? I have no idea. Just keep doing what you're doing and just keep going and see where it takes you."

Name: Geno Auriemma
Alma Mater: West Chester (1981)
Major: B.A. in Political Science
Family: Wife, Kathy, and three children, Jenna, Alyssa, and Michael
Record At UConn: 532-105 (19 seasons)
Awards: Naismith National Coach of the Year (4 times), AP National Coach of the Year (4 times), Big East Coach of the Year (6 times)

Michael McAndrews/The Hartford Courant

THREE D EFFECTS

Ann Strother gets fouled by Rebecca Richman (right) of Rutgers while Dawn McCullouch helps out on defense. Strother scored 10 points to help UConn defeat the Scarlet Knights by 25. *John Woike/The Hartford Courant*

RUTGERS OUTMATCHED BY TAURASI & CO.

By Jeff Goldberg *The Hartford Courant*

It was a shot so ugly, it would have broken mirrors, if not the backboard. Diana Taurasi launched the three-pointer with 11:24 left in the first half, and it hit the back of the rim with a thud.

Any time in the previous five games, with Taurasi's outside shot on a leave of absence, the brick would have had no chance of going in. But not this game. Not the way Taurasi had it going. The shot was deadened on the rim and fell into the basket. UConn led Rutgers by 11, and it would only increase from there.

Taurasi finished with 27 points and had her best shooting day in weeks, making 10 of 15. The fifth-ranked Huskies followed her lead and whipped Rutgers 72-47 before 16,294 at the Civic Center and a national television audience.

Taurasi (1,876 points) moved past Svetlana Abrosimova into fifth place on UConn's all-time scoring list, and UConn continued to move past the two losses that had the team and its star lacking in confidence.

"That felt good to get a couple bounces," said Taurasi, who made a career-high seven three-pointers on nine attempts. "Today we were getting a couple bounces defensively and offensively, and when you shoot and the shot goes in like that, it gives you a little bit of confidence."

Taurasi had a pregame pep talk with coach Geno Auriemma, who wanted Taurasi to be more aggressive offensively, despite her five-game stretch of 25-for-75 shooting.

Taurasi responded, making her first five shots, including three three-pointers. Her third three-pointer, with 10:29 left, gave her 13 points and the Huskies a 17-5 lead.

"She was overly concerned with the rest of the guys on the team and how they were dealing with what was going on," Auriemma said. "I think she needed to clear her mind and worry about Diana, and she did that today. The plays that she made are plays we're accustomed to seeing Diana make the last couple of years."

OPPOSITE: Willnett Crockett slices past Michelle Campbell of Rutgers on her way to scoring two of her eight points at the Hartford Civic Center. Crockett also pulled down eight rebounds and added three steals in her 15 minutes. *John Woike/The Hartford Courant*

UConn caught the Scarlet Knights at the right time. Rutgers was missing key personnel because of injuries and off-court issues, and its best player, Cappie Pondexter, perhaps tired from playing every minute in the previous three games, missed 10 straight shots in the first half.

With Rutgers missing and unable to set up its press defense, UConn rebounded and ran the Knights into submission in the first half. After scoring one fast-break basket in the previous two games combined, UConn had 12 fast-break points in the first half and led 40-17 at the half.

It was UConn's best first-half performance since the Duke game. And there was no second-half letdown. UConn led by as many as 35 in the second half.

"We really needed to come out with a statement, come out defensively, and really put the clamps down and rebound," Taurasi said. "When we rebound, we run. Today we did a good job of that."

Ann Strother had 10 points for UConn, and Willnett Crockett, whose play in the past two games has given the Huskies a new, aggressive posture in the low post, had eight points, eight rebounds and three steals. Crockett did most of her damage in the first half, as UConn raced to leads of 21-7, 28-11 and 38-13.

"We're at our best when we have a good rotation out there that includes Willnett, because Willnett changes the game when she's playing with a lot of energy," Auriemma said.

	1st	2nd	Total
Rutgers	17	30	47
UConn	40	32	72

Rutgers

Player	FGM-A	3PM-A	FTM-A	O-D REB	A	BLK	S	TP
52 A. Cahoe	1-1	0-0	0-0	0-0	0	0	0	2
55 R. Richman	4-6	0-0	0-0	2-2	0	1	0	8
25 C. Pondexter	6-24	1-6	0-0	1-1	2	0	1	13
32 C. Newton	1-4	0-0	0-0	0-2	2	0	1	2
35 D. McCullouch	2-8	1-4	2-3	2-1	2	0	2	7
00 S. Hurns	3-8	0-0	0-0	2-1	1	2	0	6
03 C. Locke	1-3	1-3	0-0	0-2	0	0	0	3
34 M. Campbell	2-7	0-0	2-4	5-2	2	0	1	6

UConn

Player	FGM-A	3PM-A	FTM-A	O-D REB	A	BLK	S	TP
33 B. Turner	3-5	0-1	0-0	0-2	2	1	0	6
43 A. Strother	4-11	2-5	0-0	1-2	2	0	0	10
31 J. Moore	1-2	0-0	3-4	2-2	1	1	0	5
03 D. Taurasi	10-15	7-9	0-0	0-4	3	0	3	27
05 M. Conlon	1-3	1-2	2-2	1-4	3	0	2	5
02 A. Valley	1-2	0-0	0-0	1-0	1	1	0	2
04 K. Robinson	0-1	0-0	0-1	0-1	1	0	0	0
12 S. Marron	1-2	0-0	0-0	0-0	0	0	0	2
20 M. Valley	0-0	0-0	0-0	1-1	1	0	0	0
22 A. Battle	1-3	0-0	2-2	2-0	1	0	1	4
23 W. Crockett	4-4	0-0	0-0	2-6	0	0	3	8
34 L. Sherwood	1-2	0-0	1-2	0-0	1	0	0	3

"She's too big, she's too quick, and she's too strong for most people to handle, and all of a sudden our defense changes and then for her to make a couple of buckets on the other end puts more gravy on top of that."

Pondexter, who played 39 minutes and made six of 24 shots, led Rutgers with 13 points.

"I am not worried at all," Pondexter said. "UConn is a top five team. They are a great team. We just have to continue to work and get healthy. This is not the end of the road."

OPPOSITE: Diana Taurasi steals the ball from Dawn McCullouch of Rutgers during the first half. Taurasi scored 27 points, including a career-high seven three-pointers, to go along with three steals, three assists and four rebounds in the victory. *John Woike/The Hartford Courant*

ANN STROTHER #43

By Jeff Goldberg   *The Hartford Courant*

The last point of last season was scored by Ann Strother. Her two free throws with 20 seconds left in the national championship game sealed the 73-68 victory over Tennessee and capped one of the best nights of her freshman year.

"She's a winner," coach Geno Auriemma said. "She makes plays to win. The behind-the-back layup last year [against Tennessee] at the Civic Center. The free throws she makes in crunch time. She knows she's good and she makes plays to win. Other kids, I think, are a little tentative. She's not tentative."

Strother has another chance to make an impact on a big game when, for the first time, Strother will play at Thompson-Boling Arena in Knoxville as No. 4 UConn faces No. 1 Tennessee in the annual steel-cage match.

"You try to prepare for every game the same, but when it comes to the big games and the noise of the crowd, it gets your energy flowing," Strother said. "I haven't played in front of [the Tennessee fans], but the way I'm thinking about going into it, I don't think it will affect me. If anything, it will add to the motivation."

Strother has been coming through in clutch situations most of her basketball life. She won back-to-back state titles at Highlands Ranch High School in Colorado and was the only high school player to make the 2001 U.S. junior national team, coached by Auriemma.

As a UConn freshman, she played the most minutes on the team and had her best games against Tennessee and Duke.

``For me, it's almost easier to play in games like that because you have the momentum going, you have everything already there for you," Strother said. "Most people might look at it as the game where everybody gets crazy. For me, it's like, 'OK, this is why you play.'"

At times in her sophomore season, Strother has struggled to assert herself in the offense. But Saturday she shot the ball the first two times she touched it. The second one went through for a three-pointer, and she never stopped looking for her shot.

"You do sense that there's a different kind of feel for her right now," Auriemma said. "But Ann goes through these streaks where for a week her shot won't even touch the rim. And then she'll go a week where everything she throws up will miss, and it starts to bother her.

"I think she's starting to understand something I'm going to have to keep reminding her: 'Ann, you're a sophomore. In the next couple of years, you're going to miss a couple shots, so don't let it bother you.' But she's on one of those kicks right now where she can't wait to shoot the ball."

It was a quick start in April that propelled Strother to her 17-point game against Tennessee. Strother had struggled throughout the postseason but hit her first three-point attempt against the Lady Vols and settled in.

"I think one of the hardest things to do as a player is get that momentum going, and to knock down that first shot really calms you down and gets you ready to go," Strother said. "I've told people, I need to do more, I need to be more aggressive, and this is the week I need to do it. Right now, I feel a lot more confident. I think it just takes time to reach that point, and I think I'm there."

Name: Ann Strother
Born: December 11, 1983
Hometown: Castle Rock, Colorado
High School: Highlands Ranch
Position: Guard
Height: 6'2"
Major: Nursing
Class: Sophomore

Bob MacDonnell/The Hartford Courant

WHISTLE STOP

A traffic jam ensues under the boards as intense rivals collide and UConn beats the Tennessee Lady Vols at Thompson-Boling Arena in Knoxville. *Patrick Murphy-Racey/WireImage.com*

UCONN SILENCES KNOXVILLE CROWD

By Jeff Goldberg *The Hartford Courant*

The UConn contingent no doubt left Thompson-Boling Arena feeling it was denied justice. But the Huskies weren't denied the victory over No. 1 Tennessee, and they have the officiating in large part to thank for it.

The officials were a major factor, sending UConn coach Geno Auriemma to the brink of sideline madness several times. Diana Taurasi fouled out of a game for the first time since her freshman season. But it was all secondary to the outcome. No. 4 UConn knocked off the Lady Vols 81-67 before 20,961, extending its winning streak over Tennessee to five games in this still-fierce rivalry.

The Huskies lead the series, 12-6.

Taurasi scored 18 points before fouling out with 46 seconds remaining. She had picked up her fourth foul with 8:01 left, and Shanna Zolman hit a three-pointer on the next possession to cut UConn's lead to 65-61.

But Tennessee would get no closer than four the rest of the way. And despite UConn's gamelong protestations against the crew of Sally Bell, John Morningstar and Wesley Dean, the Huskies put the game away from the free throw line.

Leading 67-63 with 6:28 left, UConn made seven of eight free throws over the next three minutes to take a 74-65 lead. Then Ann Strother scored on a baseline drive with 2:16 left, UConn's only field goal in the final 6:28, to put UConn up by 11.

Strother scored 17 points for UConn, matching her total from last season's national championship game against the Vols. Barbara Turner had 16 points and nine rebounds and Ashley Battle scored 11 off the bench.

Zolman and Tye'sha Fluker each had 14 for Tennessee, which had an 11-game winning streak snapped.

Taurasi made three three-pointers, the last making her UConn's all-time leading three-point shooter with 280, breaking Wendy Davis' record that had stood since 1991.

Taurasi scored her first basket Thursday with 17:55 left, hitting a three-pointer to give UConn a 6-3 lead. The first four minutes were played at a fast pace, as the officials let both teams play, not calling a foul until Turner was hit attempting a layup with 15:50 left.

But that call on Ashley Robinson opened an early floodgate of calls, with nine fouls in the next three minutes. Five were assessed to the home team, including a

OPPOSITE: Jessica Moore passes the ball as she's defended by Tennessee's Tye'Sha Fluker. *AP/WWP*

second foul on Robinson that sent the six-foot-five senior to the bench with 14:51 left in the half.

Willnett Crockett drew Robinson's second foul with an offensive rebound, and her two free throws started UConn on an 8-0 run to take a 16-9 lead. With Robinson out, UConn enjoyed a five-minute stretch of rebound dominance, holding a 6-1 edge before Robinson re-entered with 9:56 left.

Fluker had scored four straight to pull the Lady Vols to 16-13. Then Turner kept alive her own missed layup, flicking the ball out to Maria Conlon on the perimeter for a three-pointer. On UConn's next possession, Jessica Moore rebounded a missed three by Taurasi and Conlon scored again on a pull-up in the lane for a 21-13 lead.

But in a half of runs, Tennessee answered with eight straight to tie the score. Fluker, who would score 12 points in the first half, converted a three-point play, and Brittany Jackson scored five straight for a 21-21 tie.

Battle's third three-pointer of the season and Moore's post-up put UConn back up by five with 7:31 left, but Tennessee got the next five on another Fluker three-point play and two Sidney Spencer free throws with 6:39 left, courtesy of Taurasi's second foul on a reach-in from behind.

Taurasi went to the bench with 5:04 left, having missed five straight shots, but UConn scored four straight in her absence to take a 37-30 lead with 2:21 left when Taurasi checked back in.

On UConn's next possession, Taurasi hit a three from the right side, giving UConn its biggest lead at 40-30 and tying Davis with 279 three-pointers.

OPPOSITE: Tennessee's Shyra Ely, right, drives against Barbara Turner during the first half. With 16 points, Turner was one of four Huskies to score in double figures. She also led the team with nine rebounds. *AP/WWP*

	1st	2nd	Total
UConn	41	40	81
Tennessee	33	34	67

UConn

Player	FGM-A	3PM-A	FTM-A	O-D REB	A	BLK	S	TP
33 B. Turner	6-16	1-2	3-9	3-6	3	0	1	16
43 A. Strother	6-14	3-9	2-2	3-4	0	1	1	17
31 J. Moore	2-3	0-0	1-3	2-5	1	1	0	5
03 D. Taurasi	4-13	3-7	7-9	2-3	5	1	2	18
05 M. Conlon	3-6	2-4	0-1	1-2	3	0	1	8
22 A. Battle	5-12	1-1	0-0	3-2	1	0	3	11
23 W. Crockett	1-2	0-0	4-4	1-1	0	0	1	6
34 L. Sherwood	0-0	0-0	0-0	0-0	0	0	0	0

Tennessee

Player	FGM-A	3PM-A	FTM-A	O-D REB	A	BLK	S	TP
25 B. Jackson	3-9	2-5	2-2	0-0	2	0	1	10
43 S. Ely	4-9	0-0	2-2	5-9	2	0	0	10
33 A. Robinson	4-5	0-0	0-0	1-1	1	0	2	8
03 T. Butts	1-8	1-4	3-5	2-5	4	0	0	6
05 S. Zolman	5-11	2-3	2-2	1-4	3	1	0	14
01 S. Spencer	0-3	0-1	5-6	2-3	4	1	0	5
04 L. Davis	0-0	0-0	0-0	0-0	0	0	0	0
13 D. Redding	0-1	0-1	0-0	0-0	0	0	0	0
50 T. Fluker	5-10	0-0	4-4	0-4	0	3	0	14

Moore hit one of two free throws with 38.6 seconds left to complete another 8-0 run and give UConn a 41-30 lead. UConn got the ball back off a turnover with 25 seconds left and called time out to set up a final shot of the half.

But Battle inexplicably pulled up for an 18-footer with 12 seconds left and missed, giving Tennessee the last chance. Zolman capitalized, nailing a three with six seconds left to cut UConn's lead to 41-33 and send Auriemma into a rage on the sideline, pounding the seat of his chair in frustration.

He likely had a flashback to the 2001 national semifinal against Notre Dame, when an Irish three at the end of the first half triggered their second-half surge.

Tennessee began Thursday's second half in similar fashion, outscoring UConn 8-3 in the first 2:35 to close to 44-41.

MARIA CONLON #5

By Jeff Goldberg *The Hartford Courant*

It was July 2002, during UConn's summer basketball camp, and coach Geno Auriemma was looking skeptically at Maria Conlon. She was entering her third season with the program, but the first in which she would be counted on to contribute on a meaningful level. Auriemma was not convinced.

He wasn't alone. Almost from the moment Conlon signed her letter of intent with UConn in 1999, there internet chatter that the five-foot-nine guard from Derby would never make a serious impact. After her first two seasons, it seemed she had more naysayers than minutes played.

Assistant coach Tonya Cardoza had a different take. Standing next to Auriemma that July afternoon, she pointed at Conlon. "You're looking at our starting point guard next year."

"Tonya, the visionary," Auriemma said. "She was right."

"It's always good to prove people wrong and stick it to people," said Conlon. "But there's a part of me that always thought I could do it. My satisfaction is proving to myself what more I can do."

Conlon had plenty to prove the summer of 2002. Slowed by mononucleosis as a freshman and buried behind Sue Bird as a sophomore, Conlon spent that summer working out at home, readying herself for an increased role on a team integrating four freshmen.

"There comes a point where you understand it's your turn to step up," said Conlon, who averaged 3.9 points and 1.4 assists her first two seasons. "Every day that I was working out, the thought in my mind was, 'I'm going to be needed to be counted on. Whether everyone in the country thinks that's impossible, it doesn't matter. It's got to be done.'"

It still almost didn't happen. Nicole Wolff beat Conlon out for the starting point guard job, and only when Wolff's season was cut short by injury did Conlon get her chance.

"That's where her toughness came out," Auriemma said. "When Nicole got hurt, she was more than ready, because she had prepared herself for that moment."

Conlon averaged 29.7 minutes last season with 6.9 points and a two-to-one assist/turnover ratio. She was the steadying force in the backcourt, particularly in the NCAA Tournament.

To a public that knew little of the only state player on the roster, her contribution was the surprise of the season. In the locker room, it was a different story.

"We were never surprised," Taurasi said. "We knew what she could do. We all had confidence in her. We always did. When you do it day in and day out in practice, that's where you build confidence and character. She's had a great career. She's gotten the most out of her talent. That's the only thing you can say about anyone."

"You know, Maria's the favorite basher that everybody has," Auriemma said. "I'll bet she's sick of hearing it. I know I'm sick of hearing it. But then again, she's spent her whole career here proving people wrong. She was good enough to help us win a national championship last year. She'll be good enough to help us win it again."

Name: Maria Conlon
Born: November 20, 1982
Hometown: Derby, Connecticut
High School: Seymore High
School
Position: Guard
Height: 5'9"
Major: Communications Science
Class: Senior

CALL IT PASS/FAIL

OPPOSITE: Barbara Turner gets a stuffing from Miami's Shaquana Wilkins in the second half of UConn's 83-65 victory over the Hurricanes. *Michael Kodas/The Hartford Courant*

SLOPPY GAME STILL A "W"

By Jeff Goldberg *The Hartford Courant*

Gampel Pavilion hasn't been its usual friendly confines of late for Diana Taurasi and UConn. There was Bad Bounce Day against Georgetown January 10, when shots would not stay in the basket. Then there was Bad Back Day January 31 against St. John's, when Taurasi got injured and played 12 minutes. This game was Bad Pass Day. No. 4 UConn committed 33 turnovers, including 21 steals, against No. 22 Miami—numbers not reached in the Huskies' past decade of dominance.

Taurasi led the way with eight turnovers, and coach Geno Auriemma said that at one point he was looking for a vaudevillian hook to yank her off stage.

But it wasn't all bad. In fact, when the Huskies held on to the ball they did plenty of good things in an 83-65 victory.

"When we did complete more than one pass, it worked pretty well," said Taurasi, who had 21 points and six steals. "Is [the glass] half-empty or half-full? Obviously, I look at it as empty. We always end up kind of kicking ourselves in the butt somehow, or some way

in every game, which I guess is good because you need something to complain about."

The Huskies' greatest fear coming into the game was an emotional letdown after Thursday's win against Tennessee. But UConn came out with an overabundance of energy. It paid off in the paint, where the Huskies had a 46-30 rebounding advantage, and it fueled an aggressive defense. It also translated well to their shooting. The Huskies were 30 of 57 (52.6 percent), their most accurate performance in the past five games.

"It could have been a lot worse, and we did do some good things," Taurasi said. "The defense in the first half, we kept them under wraps. I think the rebounding was good, and when we completed passes we got the shots we wanted."

But those turnovers. UConn had 19 in the first half. The Huskies played at a speed beyond their ability, try-

OPPOSITE: The UConn Women were plagued by turnovers during the game against Miami, but Jessica Moore got one back when she made this steal from Miami's Yalonda McCormick during the first half. *Michael Kodas/The Hartford Courant*

RIGHT: Ashley Battle heads for the hoop in the second half of UConn's game against Miami. Battle came off the bench to score 18 points.
Michael Kodas/The Hartford Courant

ing to force the knockout blow after taking a quick 18-9 lead. Maria Conlon had a career-high seven turnovers after having six in the previous eight games.

"You know, minus the turnovers, it was an unbelievably good game by us," Auriemma said. "But that's like saying 'Minus Cindy Crawford's body and her face, she's an average person.' That was a big damn part of the game."

Ashley Battle had a career-high 18 points for UConn, giving her four straight double-figure games. Jessica Moore, who had a total of 13 points in the past five games, had 13 points and 10 rebounds for her second double-double of the season. Ann Strother had 17 points for the second straight game.

UConn put it away with a 14-2 run in the second half, highlighted by back-to-back three-point plays by Battle, that gave UConn a 58-33 lead.

"When we held on to the ball, we played awesome," Battle said. "Awesome offense. We executed it really well when we didn't turn the ball over. I guess we've got to not turn the ball over."

What saved the Huskies was the Hurricanes' inability to make the turnovers count on the scoreboard. Miami, which has lost three straight, had 20 points off UConn's turnovers.

Chanivia Broussard led Miami with 20 points. Tamara James had 19.

	1st	2nd	Total
Miami	25	40	65
UConn	40	43	83

Miami

PLAYER	FGM-A	3PTM-A	FTM-A	O-D REB	A	BK	S	PTS
03 M. Knight	3-8	0-4	0-0	3-2	1	0	2	6
23 S. Wilkins	4-9	0-0	5-5	3-5	2	1	4	13
53 C. Broussard	8-18	0-1	4-6	1-2	3	1	3	20
02 T. James	6-15	3-6	4-4	1-1	2	1	7	19
10 Y. McCormick	1-14	0-6	1-2	2-2	5	0	3	3
05 I. Dhahabu	2-4	0-0	0-0	1-2	0	0	2	4
22 F. Phanord	0-0	0-0	0-0	0-0	0	0	0	0
30 H. Wilson	0-0	0-0	0-0	0-0	1	0	0	0

UConn

PLAYER	FGM-A	3PTM-A	FTM-A	O-D REB	A	BK	S	PTS
33 B. Turner	2-5	0-0	1-2	0-5	5	0	0	5
43 A. Strother	6-15	2-9	3-4	2-4	3	3	1	17
31 J. Moore	6-7	0-0	1-3	3-7	3	0	1	13
03 D. Taurasi	7-12	3-5	4-4	3-4	3	0	6	21
05 M. Conlon	0-2	0-2	0-0	1-3	4	0	2	0
02 A. Valley	0-3	0-2	0-0	0-0	3	0	0	0
04 K. Robinson	0-0	0-0	0-0	0-0	0	0	0	0
12 S. Marron	0-0	0-0	0-0	0-0	0	0	0	0
20 M. Valley	0-1	0-0	1-2	0-1	1	0	0	1
22 A. Battle	5-7	0-0	8-8	2-3	2	0	1	18
23 W. Crockett	2-2	0-0	0-1	0-3	0	0	1	4
34 L. Sherwood	2-3	0-0	0-0	1-1	0	0	1	4

"We weren't patient, we didn't run our offense, and we ended up taking quick shots and bad shots," Miami coach Ferne Labati said. "And then we got Connecticut to turn the ball over and we didn't capitalize on it and turned the ball over ourselves. We really didn't benefit on the turnovers."

Shea Comes Home

Shea Ralph and Geno Auriemma catch up before the tip-off as the Huskies faced Ralph's Pittsburgh Panthers at the Civic Center. UConn defeated the Panthers 97-42. *John Woike/The Hartford Courant*

HUSKIES DOMINATE PANTHERS

By Jeff Goldberg *The Hartford Courant*

This was not a fair fight, and both teams knew it. It was about the game within the game for both No. 2 UConn and an overmatched Pittsburgh team. It had to be that way because the game itself was so one-sided.

UConn scored 56 points in the first half, the most since getting 56 against Pittsburgh on January 2, 2002, and defeated the Panthers 97-42 before 16,294 at the Civic Center.

It was the most points and largest margin of victory for the Huskies this season.

But more important to the defending national champions was that they had continued their best stretch of basketball this season, just three weeks before the start of the postseason.

"We're cruising right now," said Ashley Battle, who led the Huskies with 15 points. "We're playing really good basketball, and if we keep this up, the sky's the limit."

Maybe a month ago, when UConn was struggling to redefine itself after losses to Duke and Notre Dame, a team as mismatched as Pittsburgh could have stayed with the Huskies for long stretches.

But not now. The Huskies led 17-13 with 13:00 left in the first half; then, like a cat batting at a mouse, the Huskies tired of the game and went for the kill. They outscored Pittsburgh 39-8 the rest of the half to take a 56-21 lead. With 10:18 left in the game, it was 80-27. The Huskies established their largest lead of the season at 57 points with 2:03 remaining.

UConn won with defense, forcing Pittsburgh into 24 turnovers and scoring a season-high 38 points off of them. UConn also had a season-high 18 steals.

On offense, the Huskies made a season-high 12 three-pointers and committed just nine turnovers.

"If you're just going out there to win the game and don't care about how you play, you pass up an opportunity to prepare for down the road," UConn coach Geno Auriemma said. "Regardless of the talent level Pittsburgh had, we played in such a way that we made ourselves feel good about it. Final score didn't matter. We feel like we accomplished something."

OPPOSITE: Diana Taurasi is all business as she pushes the ball upcourt against Pittsburgh. Taurasi finished with 11 points, eight assists, six rebounds, two steals and a block during the Huskies' victory. *John Woike/The Hartford Courant*

No UConn starter played more than 22 minutes, and the bench accounted for 56 points.

Freshman Liz Sherwood had a career-high 14 points. Diana Taurasi had 11 points, eight assists and six rebounds. Barbara Turner had 10 points. It was the fifth straight game in which UConn had four players in double figures.

UConn used all 12 of its players in the first half, and 10 had at least three points.

"Everyone got in, and the level of intensity stayed the same throughout," said Ann Strother, who had nine points on three three-pointers. "That's a good sign of a great team. Everyone's playing really well right now. Everyone is picking it up a lot."

Pittsburgh is rebuilding with a new coaching staff—including former UConn All-American Shea Ralph—and a young lineup lacking experience. They came into Tuesday's game having lost eight straight and were without second leading scorer Jessica Allen from New London High School, who is out with a stress fracture in her left foot.

For Pitt, it was a night to recognize little victories, including winning the opening jump ball.

"We won in a couple of areas, small areas," Pittsburgh coach Agnus Berenato said. "I felt like the first five or six minutes we competed, but then I think we weren't able to get anything accomplished."

Katie Histed and Jennifer Brown led Pittsburgh with 12 points each.

It was a bittersweet return for Ralph, who played at UConn from 1996-01 and was the 2000 Final Four MVP.

She received a warm welcome during introductions before the game.

"It was great to see them play well," Ralph said. "I know they've struggled in a couple of games this year. It was exactly how I remember it. I just think they're really playing well, and now is when you want to peak."

	1st	2nd	Total
Pittsburgh	21	21	42
UConn	56	41	97

Pittsburgh

Player	FGM-A	3PM-A	FTM-A	O-D REB	A	BLK	S	TP
45 L. Kincaid	2-3	0-0	2-3	0-2	1	0	0	6
54 S. Stufflet	0-2	0-0	0-0	0-0	0	0	0	0
55 A. Morris	2-5	0-0	0-0	0-3	0	0	0	4
22 A. Kunich	1-4	1-3	0-0	0-2	3	0	1	3
30 K. Histed	5-13	2-4	0-0	1-1	0	1	1	12
03 J. Brown	5-11	0-0	2-5	3-2	0	4	0	12
10 B. Hughes	0-1	0-0	0-0	1-1	0	0	0	0
24 S. Moore	0-1	0-0	0-0	2-1	1	0	2	0
35 B. Larkin	0-0	0-0	0-0	0-0	0	0	0	0
44 D. Taylor	1-6	1-3	0-0	1-0	0	0	0	3
52 C. Taylor	0-1	0-0	2-2	0-0	0	0	2	2

UConn

Player	FGM-A	3PM-A	FTM-A	O-D REB	A	BLK	S	TP
33 B. Turner	3-5	2-2	2-4	2-1	1	0	1	10
43 A. Strother	3-10	3-6	0-0	1-1	1	0	1	9
31 J. Moore	2-3	0-0	1-2	1-5	1	0	2	5
03 D. Taurasi	4-7	3-5	0-0	3-3	8	1	2	11
05 M. Conlon	2-3	2-3	0-0	0-0	5	0	0	6
02 A. Valley	3-3	0-0	1-3	0-1	5	0	5	7
04 K. Robinson	2-7	1-2	2-2	2-4	0	0	0	7
12 S. Marron	1-2	1-2	0-0	0-0	1	0	0	3
20 M. Valley	1-2	0-0	0-0	1-0	2	0	1	2
22 A. Battle	7-8	0-0	1-1	2-2	1	0	5	15
23 W. Crockett	3-5	0-0	2-5	4-3	1	0	1	8
34 L. Sherwood	6-7	0-0	2-4	1-0	0	0	0	14

OPPOSITE: Willnett Crockett is fouled by Jennifer Brown of Pittsburgh as Bridget Larkin closes in. The UConn bench outscored their Panther counterparts 56-17 during the game. *John Woike/The Hartford Courant*

DIANA TAURASI #3

By Jeff Goldberg *The Hartford Courant*

She wasn't born until after Nancy Lieberman's career was over. She grew up in California, but was too young to remember Cheryl Miller. Her college career began a few months after Chamique Holdsclaw's ended.

Like those three superstars before her, Taurasi has played the game of basketball unlike any of her peers or many of her predecessors. Is she the greatest women's player of all-time?

"To say that about one player I think is a little much, no matter how good they are," Taurasi said. "Every generation has their own great players."

Perhaps that is true. But in four years at Connecticut, with 2,121 points, four Final Fours, three national championships and countless spectacular moments along the way, she has earned her place among the best ever.

Nancy Lieberman played before there was an NCAA Tournament, before there was ESPN. But in the mid to late 1970s, Lieberman was a one-woman force in women's basketball, a three-time Kodak All-American who led Old Dominion to two AIWA national titles and ultimately earned a tryout with the NBA's Indiana Pacers.

"She was a 'play like a guy' player," said Mel Greenberg, the venerable women's basketball writer for the *Philadelphia Inquirer* and godfather of the AP women's poll. "The thing about Nancy...the game would start, Nancy would...give someone a shot to the throat and it's like, 'I ain't guarding her the rest of the game.' It was pure New York playground mentality and toughness, making key shots."

Everyone knows about Reggie Miller's brashness and on-court theatrics. But he was just copying the original showman, his sister Cheryl. The USC star who played from 1982-86 was the women's basketball answer to the Lakers' Showtime.

Miller scored 3,018 points in her career and won the Naismith trophy three times, leading USC to two NCAA titles. And she did it with a style and flair that can be seen in Taurasi's game.

"There's a healthy comparison to Cheryl Miller because there's a fire and a passion about Diana's game that people get wrapped up in," Ann Donovan, who won one of those titles with Lieberman in 1980, said. "Cheryl had that going for her, besides a skill level, there was a passion for the game that Diana has."

The next really big thing was down in Tennessee. Chamique Holdsclaw changed the game again, leading the Lady Vols to an unprecedented three straight titles from 1996-98. She was the first three-time AP first-team All-American. Holdsclaw is the only 3,000-point scorer in Tennessee history and their leading rebounder with 1,295.

Lieberman, Miller and Holdsclaw broke the mold in their eras. Now Taurasi joins them as the sport's Fantastic Four.

"I don't know of anybody else in 30 years I've been coaching that has the offensive skills from long range and the ability to make big plays for herself and other people," Vols coach Pat Summitt said. "I just think she's been the best at making the big plays, night in and night out. Impact on the women's game is the way I look at it. And when I look at Diana's impact, it's huge."

Name: Diana Taurasi
Born: June 11, 1982
Hometown: Chino, California
High School: Don Lugo High School
Position: Guard
Height: 6'0"
Major: Communications Science
Class: Senior

A SHARE OF FIRST

Maria Conlon and Diana Taurasi have some fun with each other during the game against Providence College. Taurasi fell short of scoring her 2000th point, scoring only six points in 23 minutes. *Bob MacDonnell/The Hartford Courant*

UCONN IS SHARE HOLDER

By Jeff Goldberg *The Hartford Courant*

Last season, UConn's game at Providence in March was a big red flag for the Huskies. They were lethargic in an 18-point victory, and things went so poorly that Diana Taurasi was benched at the start of the second half.

Ten days later, the Huskies were handed their only loss of the season. This time, it was a big white flag for the Friars.

The top-ranked Huskies hit Providence with a 30-0 run in the first half, and all that was left was to fill in the final score: UConn 79, Providence 38.

UConn clinched a share of the regular-season championship, extending its streak of conference titles to 11.

"Last year at this time, going down to the Big East tournament, we had struggled for two or three weeks," UConn coach Geno Auriemma said. "We were winning, but we weren't exactly happy. Right now we're in a pretty good frame of mind. We're winning and we're happy and we're playing well."

Providence is last in the conference, and there was little chance the Friars could prevent UConn's 12th victory in a row.

The Huskies wasted no time putting the game away, scoring 30 straight points in just under 11 minutes to take a 35-4 lead with 8:16 left in the half. The Huskies made 13 of their first 17 shots and had assists on all 13. UConn led 45-16 at the half, its third largest halftime margin of the season.

The 30-0 run was UConn's largest since scoring 30 straight at Wright State on December 31, 2001.

"It's difficult to play in these games," Auriemma said. "How can you come out looking good in a game like this? But I thought we did come out looking good. We wanted to execute our stuff, and for the most part we did."

Ann Strother led UConn with 10 points. The Huskies had their string of games with four double-digit scorers snapped at six. But only three Huskies played more than 17 minutes, and UConn had five players with at least eight points.

OPPOSITE: Ann Strother struggles to get a shot off over Jill Furstenburg during the first half of the 41-point UConn win at Gampel Pavillion. *Bob MacDonnell/The Hartford Courant*

Maria Conlon had nine points on three three-pointers to move into sixth place on UConn's all-time list with 153. Jessica Moore had nine points and 10 rebounds. Barbara Turner also had nine points.

Taurasi, who needed 14 points to become the fifth UConn player to reach 2,000 for her career, had six in 23 minutes. But she had a season-high 10 assists—two shy of her career high—and needs 40 to tie Jen Rizzotti's school record of 537.

"I don't want to go into games just wanting to score to break a record," said Taurasi, who has 1,992 points, 186 behind Nykesha Sales' school record. "There are a lot of games where I'll score, but right now it's really not necessary."

Providence made its first two shots and trailed 5-4 after 65 seconds. The Huskies then went on their run as the Friars missed 12 straight shots and committed seven turnovers.

Taurasi made her first basket with 11:56 left, and Conlon followed with her third three-pointer as UConn's lead ballooned to 29-4. UConn was 11 for 15 and Taurasi had six of UConn's 11 assists.

"Right now we're on a great roll defensively and offensively," Taurasi said. "A lot of people have clear minds and it's going well."

OPPOSITE: **Liz Sherwood battles to keep control of the ball in the paint as she is pressured by Shauna Snyder (left) and Jama Gilmore during the first half.** *Bob MacDonnell/The Hartford Courant*

	1st	2nd	Total
Providence	16	22	38
UConn	45	34	79

Providence

Player	FGM-A	3PM-A	FTM-A	O-D REB	A	BLK	S	TP
30 G. Nwafili	2-9	0-0	0-0	2-0	1	1	1	4
02 K. Baugh	3-6	1-1	0-0	0-3	1	0	1	7
14 J. Furstenburg	2-9	0-2	1-2	1-5	3	0	1	5
23 K. Quinn	0-2	0-2	0-0	0-1	0	0	0	0
42 B. Freeburg	1-5	0-0	1-2	0-0	1	0	1	3
24 S. Snyder	3-14	1-7	0-0	0-3	1	0	2	7
35 J. Gilmore	4-11	0-0	0-0	1-4	2	0	0	8
40 K. Keefe	2-3	0-1	0-0	2-1	2	0	0	4

UConn

Player	FGM-A	3PM-A	FTM-A	O-D REB	A	BLK	S	TP
33 B. Turner	4-6	0-1	1-2	0-2	1	0	2	9
43 A. Strother	4-6	2-3	0-2	2-4	2	0	1	10
31 J. Moore	4-6	0-0	1-3	3-7	1	0	0	9
03 D. Taurasi	2-6	2-6	0-0	0-3	10	0	2	6
05 M. Conlon	3-6	3-6	0-0	0-1	3	0	0	9
02 A. Valley	0-1	0-1	1-2	0-3	2	0	0	1
04 K. Robinson	3-6	1-2	0-0	2-0	2	0	0	7
12 S. Marron	2-2	1-1	0-0	0-1	0	0	0	5
22 A. Battle	1-5	0-2	2-2	0-4	1	0	1	4
23 W. Crockett	4-4	0-0	0-0	1-1	1	1	0	8
34 L. Sherwood	2-4	0-0	3-6	2-4	0	2	0	7
20 M. Valley	2-4	0-0	0-0	0-3	3	0	0	4

GOOD NIGHT FROM STORRS

Diana Taurasi and Meg Bulger of West Virginia battle for a loose ball Senior Night. The UConn women celebrated Senior Night with a 28-point victory. *John Woike/The Hartford Courant*

LAST GAME AT GAMPEL IS ROUT

By Jeff Goldberg *The Hartford Courant*

They are 132-7 in their careers. They have been to the Final Four three times and have won two national championships.

Diana Taurasi, Maria Conlon and Morgan Valley know what it means to rise to the occasion. So it was only fitting that on a night held in their honor, the Huskies rose to lofty heights one more time. The three seniors made their final game at Gampel Pavilion memorable. Fourth-ranked UConn erased all evidence of the stumble at Villanova by routing unranked West Virginia 100-72 before an emotional crowd of 10,167 on Senior Night.

"I think we played the way we wanted to play," said Taurasi, who had her first double-double of the season with 17 points and 10 assists. "And there's no better night to do that than Senior Night. This team thrives on games like this. For the next nine, we need to play like this."

It was a rousing conclusion to the regular season. UConn had a season-high six players in double figures

and reached its season high in points with 2:22 remaining. It was the first time UConn hit the century mark since scoring 109 against Pepperdine in December 2002.

The Huskies matched a season high with 56 points in the first half, capped by Taurasi's pull-up three-pointer from 25 feet at the buzzer. UConn's total for the game was 56.

Conlon, who tied her career high for three-pointers with four—all in the first half—finished with 12 points, five assists and five rebounds. Valley had two points and three rebounds in her first start of the season.

"For the most part, tonight went according to plan," coach Geno Auriemma said. "The script was for Maria to make a lot of threes...for D to make that bomb. Morgan would do the things Morgan does. It was one of those Senior Nights where they got to enjoy the things

---

OPPOSITE: Maria Conlon stretches out to defend a shot by Yolanda Paige of West Virginia. Conlon scored 12 points and handed out five assists on the night to help the Huskies to a 100-72 victory. *John Woike/The Hartford Courant*

they've always enjoyed for the four years they've been here."

UConn had as many as five players in double figures just one other time this season—at West Virginia on Jan. 7.

Jessica Moore, who played just 12 minutes against Villanova after getting elbowed in the mouth, had 20 points and nine rebounds. Ann Strother had 15 points, while Barbara Turner and Wilnett Crockett each scored 14. Crockett tied her career high.

UConn outrebounded the Mountaineers 52-20 with Turner (12) leading the way.

Sherell Sowho led West Virginia with 24 points. Meg Bulger scored 21. It was the first time this season UConn allowed as many as 70 points.

Because NCAA Tournament first- and second-round games will be played in Bridgeport this season instead of Gampel, the pregame ceremony took on added significance.

The ceremony was as much a celebration as a tearful farewell. Taurasi, Conlon and Valley have a chance to be the fifth, sixth and seventh players in women's basketball history to play in four straight Final Fours.

Jay Valley, Morgan's father, set the tone for the 15-minute ceremony, putting on sunglasses as he walked his daughter to midcourt, hoping to hide his tears. The glasses quickly came off, and the tears flowed. Even Conlon and Taurasi, usually the most stoic players on the roster, were misty-eyed as they received framed jerseys and hugged Auriemma amid vigorous standing ovations.

OPPOSITE: Jessica Moore takes a forearm to the nose as she spins towards the hoop. Moore scored 20 points and grabbed nine rebounds. *John Woike/The Hartford Courant*

	1st	2nd	Total
West Virginia	36	36	72
UConn	56	44	100

West Virginia

Player	FGM-A	3PM-A	FTM-A	O-D REB	A	BLK	S	TP
05 M. Carter	0-2	0-0	0-0	0-0	0	0	1	0
34 J. Dunlap	1-3	0-0	0-0	1-2	1	0	0	2
12 Y. Paige	2-12	0-0	3-4	0-1	6	0	0	7
14 S. Sowho	8-18	6-13	2-2	1-1	3	1	2	24
42 K. Bulger	5-17	4-9	0-0	0-2	2	0	1	14
04 M. Bulger	8-13	2-4	3-3	0-4	1	0	2	21
10 K. Glusko	0-0	0-0	2-2	0-0	0	0	0	2
21 L. Williams	1-2	0-0	0-0	0-0	0	0	0	2
23 L. Costello	0-0	0-0	0-0	0-0	0	0	0	0

UConn

Player	FGM-A	3PM-A	FTM-A	O-D REB	A	BLK	S	TP
20 M. Valley	1-2	0-0	0-0	2-1	2	0	0	2
22 A. Battle	1-5	0-0	0-0	1-1	4	0	2	2
31 J. Moore	9-12	0-1	2-4	4-5	0	0	0	20
03 D. Taurasi	6-16	3-9	2-2	0-4	10	1	0	17
05 M. Conlon	4-6	4-5	0-0	1-4	5	0	0	12
02 A. Valley	0-0	0-0	0-0	0-1	1	0	0	0
04 K. Robinson	0-0	0-0	1-2	0-1	0	0	0	1
12 S. Marron	0-0	0-0	0-0	0-0	0	0	0	0
23 W. Crockett	6-8	0-0	2-3	2-5	0	1	0	14
33 B. Turner	6-7	0-1	2-3	3-9	3	1	0	14
34 L. Sherwood	1-2	0-0	1-2	1-0	0	1	0	3
43 A. Strother	5-9	3-5	2-2	1-2	4	1	0	15

"You know it's going to be sad, but you have no clue about the emotions," Morgan Valley said. "I've been here four years and it's gone by so fast, I can't believe it."

The starting lineup featured the three seniors and redshirt juniors Jessica Moore and Ashley Battle—the class that came in together in 2000.

After a West Virginia three-pointer on the opening possession, the Huskies scored the next 11 points and the rout was on. UConn had leads of 24-12, 38-20 and 48-23.

"It could have been scripted any way tonight and it would have been special," Conlon said.

Diana Taurasi's mom Lily gets a hug from Geno Auriemma while Diana and her dad Mario look on during Senior Night ceremonies.
John Woike/The Hartford Courant

WIN PUTS COACH IN FOUL MOOD

Barbara Turner forces a turnover from Virginia Tech's center Megan Finnerty. *Michael McAndrews/The Hartford Courant*

HUSKIES WIN LOW-SCORING MATCHUP

By Jeff Goldberg *The Hartford Courant*

There was plenty of frustration to go around at the Civic Center.

There was general frustration experienced by players for UConn and Virginia Tech, unable to score against rugged defensive pressure applied by both teams. Top-seeded UConn defeated No. 8 Virginia Tech 48-34 before 10,833 in the Big East quarterfinals, the lowest-scoring game in the tournament's history. UConn's 48 points were the second lowest by a winning team. Rutgers beat Virginia Tech 44-43 in the 2002 first round.

"A win is a win," said UConn center Jessica Moore, who had 11 points. "I learned that in high school. It doesn't matter how it looks. You can bounce the ball off your head. As long as it goes in, it doesn't matter."

And then there was the acute frustration of UConn coach Geno Auriemma, generated by an unlikely source: his star player Diana Taurasi. Unlikely, perhaps, to anyone other than Auriemma.

The Big East Player of the Year, expected to lead the Huskies back to another tournament title, was of little help to her team, scoring four points in 23 minutes.

With 7:54 left in the game, she picked up her third foul. Then, in her own moment of frustration over that call, Taurasi picked up her fourth foul 17 seconds later, running right through Tech's Megan Finnerty, who was setting a screen.

And when Auriemma barked at Taurasi on the bench for her foolish fouling, Taurasi barked right back. And that proved the biggest frustration foul of all. Auriemma benched her the rest of the game, even as the Hokies cut a 14-point deficit to nine with 4:51 left.

"D hasn't fouled anybody in four years," Auriemma said. "She has not been wrong in four years, and I'm just sick of it. You don't sit there and argue with me. Nobody argues with me on the bench. Jen [Rizzotti] never did. Nykesha [Sales] never did. Svetlana [Abrosimova] would never do that, as much as I would bust her chops about it. When they were wrong, those guys knew they were wrong. This kid hasn't been wrong in four years, and it's catching up to her. I'd rather lose than let kids get away with that."

ABOVE: Jessica Moore and Ann Strother double-team Hokies forward Ieva Kublina in the second half of the Big East Tournament quarterfinal. *Michael McAndrews/The Hartford Courant*

UConn 48 | Virginia Tech 34

Auriemma's displeasure carried into the interview room. When the first three questions were for Taurasi—non-benching related—Auriemma cut in.

"How about a question for somebody who actually got something done today?" Auriemma said.

Those questions would be for Ashley Battle and Moore. Battle, who went scoreless in the first half, scored UConn's only seven points in a stretch of 9:13 in the second half, helping the Huskies maintain a double-digit lead.

Her three-point play with 4:33 left restored UConn's lead to 12, and when Moore and Barbara Turner (13 points) completed an 8-0 run, the Huskies led 46-29 with 2:46 left.

"Just grind it out," Battle said. "That's been our approach all year."

UConn scored its fewest points of the season, but held Virginia Tech to the second lowest total in program history—and that included five points in the final 40 seconds, with UConn offering token defense.

The Hokies, who were tied at 10-10 with 13:39 left in the first half, had five field goals over the next 33 minutes against UConn's zone. Carrie Mason led Virginia Tech with 13 points. Ieva Kublina had eight.

At the other end, the Huskies seemed unsure how to attack Tech's physical man-to-man defense, and when they did get open looks, their shots rimmed out. UConn shot 31.6 percent (18-for-57), its second worst effort of the season.

"We're really happy about our defense, and then at the same time, the offense wasn't there," Moore said.

	1st	2nd	Total
Virginia Tech	14	20	34
UConn	21	27	48

Virginia Tech

Player	FGM-A	3PM-A	FTM-A	O-D REB	A	BLK	S	TP
32 K. Gardin	2-8	0-0	0-2	2-3	0	0	0	4
54 E. Gibson	2-6	0-0	0-0	1-5	1	1	0	4
14 I. Kublina	2-8	0-3	4-4	1-4	0	1	0	8
23 D. Chriss	1-7	0-0	2-2	2-3	1	0	2	4
24 C. Mason	4-11	2-5	3-5	0-1	1	0	1	13
05 K. Copeland	0-2	0-0	0-0	1-1	1	0	0	0
45 M. Finnerty	0-1	0-0	1-2	0-3	0	0	0	1

UConn

Player	FGM-A	3PM-A	FTM-A	O-D REB	A	BLK	S	TP
33 B. Turner	5-12	0-2	3-3	1-3	1	0	0	13
43 A. Strother	3-9	2-4	0-0	2-2	3	1	1	8
31 J. Moore	4-6	0-0	3-4	1-3	1	0	2	11
03 D. Taurasi	2-10	0-5	0-0	1-1	3	0	2	4
05 M. Conlon	2-8	1-4	0-0	2-3	3	1	1	5
22 A. Battle	2-9	0-0	3-3	3-7	0	0	2	7
23 W. Crockett	0-2	0-0	0-0	2-1	0	0	1	0
34 L. Sherwood	0-1	0-0	0-0	1-0	0	0	0	0

"But we were able to keep it going and not get frustrated too much.

"One of the hardest things that we can possibly do in basketball is be willing to take punches from the other team and then just go right back at them. That shows how much we've grown up. I don't know if we would have been able to do that last year at this time."

OPPOSITE: Diana Taurasi blocks Hokies forward Kerri Gargin, but is called for her second foul. Taurasi had four fouls in 23 minutes. *Michael McAndrews/The Hartford Courant*

BOSTON COLLEGE KNOCKS OFF UCONN

Coach Geno Auriemma complains about a call and associ-ate head coach Chris Dailey pleads the case. *Michael McAndrews/The Hartford Courant*

HUSKIES OUT OF BIG EAST TOURNEY

By Jeff Goldberg *The Hartford Courant*

Jessalyn Deveny, an All-Big East guard, scored 21 points, including two free throws with five seconds left to give Boston College its final points. Deveny went to the line after making the play of the game, knocking down an entry pass by Ann Strother with 6.2 seconds left, then calling time out after she dove for the ball.

"I always get ragged on for my defense by Coach [Cathy Inglese]," Deveny said. "I was in the passing lane and got the ball and I was like, 'Whoa.' I knew we had it. We just had to get the ball inbounds, get fouled and put our foul shot in. We did that and it was a great win."

UConn erased an 11-point deficit late in the half to take a 65-64 lead with 4:28 left.

"In the second half, I thought we worked our butts off defensively to get back into the game," Diana Taurasi said. "Whenever you put yourself in a hole in the first half, it's never easy."

Taurasi was a factor after her benching against Virginia Tech. She scored 17 points, including a three-point play on a runner with 1:14 left that tied the score at 70. It was UConn's last basket.

The Huskies' Ashley Battle, an unlikely three-point shooter, hit a four-point play with one minute left in the first half, making a three from the corner and getting fouled by Maureen Leahy. Battle's points cut the lead to seven.

The final 26 seconds were not kind to Strother. With UConn trailing 71-70, Strother missed a three-pointer with 16 seconds left, then turned the ball over with 6.2 seconds left after Taurasi got the rebound. With five seconds left and UConn down three, Strother dribbled the ball off Jessica Moore's foot and lost control, allowing the clock to run out before the Huskies could get off a shot.

Boston College got—and made—open shots throughout the game, shooting a tournament-record 63 percent, 69.2 percent in the first half.

OPPOSITE: Ann Strother reacts after Boston College forward Brooke Queenan slapped away the ball. *Michael McAndrews/The Hartford Courant*

"Any time somebody makes a shot, it's a function of two things," UConn coach Geno Auriemma said. "You executed pretty well and the defense didn't react accordingly. But you still have to make the shots, and they did."

The Taurasi family came 3,000 miles from Chino, California, to see Diana play her final Big East tournament.

They left with disappointment after the loss. But Lily Taurasi, Diana's mother, said there were no ill feelings toward Auriemma after his benching of her daughter, which took place directly in front of them.

"That's OK," Lily said. "Oh yeah, it was OK. That's normal, you know. If you're the coach, you would do the same thing. You would act the same."

The Taurasis had dinner at the Auriemma home the night of the game—the first time they had been there since Taurasi's recruiting visit in 1999. Basketball was never a topic.

"We had a nice beautiful dinner. It was wonderful," Lily said. "My husband [Mario] spoke Italian with Geno about music, about Italy. Nothing about basketball. For Geno and Diana, it's basketball all the time. You go home and you don't talk about basketball. We had a wonderful time."

	1st	2nd	Total
Boston College	39	34	73
UConn	32	38	70

Boston College

Player	FGM-A	3PM-A	FTM-A	O-D REB	A	BLK	S	TP
11 K. Ress	8-11	0-0	2-4	4-0	1	0	1	18
15 C. Droesch	2-9	2-3	2-2	1-1	4	0	0	8
25 M. Leahy	2-3	0-0	0-0	0-1	0	1	1	4
00 J. Deveny	8-13	2-4	3-4	1-1	3	0	1	21
23 A. Jacobs	5-6	1-1	2-2	0-2	5	0	1	13
02 B. Queenan	3-3	0-0	0-0	0-1	2	0	0	6
03 S. Marshall	0-0	0-0	0-0	0-0	0	0	0	0
20 A. Parham	1-1	0-0	1-2	1-1	0	0	1	3

UConn

Player	FGM-A	3PM-A	FTM-A	O-D REB	A	BLK	S	TP
33 B. Turner	4-8	0-0	4-6	1-3	5	0	3	12
43 A. Strother	2-7	1-3	2-2	0-2	1	0	1	7
31 J. Moore	5-6	0-0	0-0	3-2	1	0	0	10
03 D. Taurasi	6-13	2-7	3-3	1-1	6	2	0	17
05 M. Conlon	4-6	2-4	0-0	0-0	1	0	2	10
02 A. Valley	0-0	0-0	0-0	0-0	1	0	0	0
20 M. Valley	0-0	0-0	0-0	0-0	0	0	0	0
22 A. Battle	3-4	1-1	1-1	1-0	1	0	0	8
23 W. Crockett	3-3	0-0	0-0	1-2	2	0	1	6

"Whenever you put yourself in a hole in the first half, it's never easy."

—Diana Taurasi

OPPOSITE: Jessica Moore is double-teamed by Kathrin Ress and Brooke Queenan. In spite of the fierce coverage, Moore scored 10 points in the game. *Michael McAndrews/The Hartford Courant*

DOMINANCE

UConn fans wish Geno Auriemma a happy birthday during the Huskies' second-round NCAA tournament game against Auburn at Harbor Yard. His team also gave him a nice present as UConn beat Auburn 79-53. *Bob MacDonnell/The Hartford Courant*

BARBARA TURNER OVERDRIVE

By Jeff Goldberg *The Hartford Courant*

During a practice session open to the public, UConn's guards put on a three-point show at one end of the court, and the crowd of roughly 5,000 cheered each basket.

At the other end, UConn's post players went through their drills almost unnoticed. They saved their show for game time. Taller, stronger and more agile than their counterparts from Penn, UConn's inside players dominated the paint. Barbara Turner posting up and Jessica Moore driving the lane were the only highlights the Huskies needed.

Turner scored 17 points, all in the first half, and Moore had 15 as UConn opened defense of the NCAA championship with a 91-55 victory before a sellout crowd of 9,091 at the Arena at Harbor Yard.

"If we can keep this going with everyone contributing and playing as a team ... now it's all coming back, slowly but surely," Moore said. "I don't think we really had our A game today, but we're getting back to what it can be."

UConn's 91 points matched its opening-round total against Boston University a year ago, when the Huskies shook off a Big East tournament loss and went on to their second straight national championship.

UConn (26-4), the No. 2 seed in the East Regional, will play next No. 7 Auburn (22-8), who defeated North Carolina State 79-59.

For Turner, a sophomore who made seven of 11 shots in the first half, her 17 points were a career NCAA Tournament high. Penn coach Kelly Greenberg said that Turner was stronger than the entire Quakers roster, and Turner proved her right, posting up at will and scoring on a variety of inside moves.

Moore, a junior, was equally effective, collecting 11 rebounds for her first NCAA Tournament double-double. Moore scored UConn's first points on a foul line jumper and drove for a three-point play at the start of a 9-0 run as UConn outscored Penn 45-17 over the final 15:42 of the first half to make it 51-23.

OPPOSITE: Jessica Moore grabs a rebound over Penn's Jennifer Fleischer (left) and Jewel Clark. Moore pulled down 11 rebounds to go with her 18 points.
Bob MacDonnell/The Hartford Courant

ABOVE: Penn guard Joey Rhoads closely follows Diana Taurasi in the opening round of the NCAA Tournament. Taurasi led all scorers with 18 points. *Michael McAndrews/The Hartford Courant*

"Coach really put the pressure on us and told us that the post players need to have a big game," Moore said. "Not only for this game, but throughout the entire tournament. We really need to make a big post presence, and I think when me and Barbara can start the game off on the right foot, it feeds that energy to everyone else on the court."

Diana Taurasi, who averaged 26.2 points in last season's tournament, had 18 points Sunday to become UConn's all-time NCAA Tournament scorer with 328 and the fourth leading scorer in tournament history. Kara Wolters (1994-97) had held the UConn record with 322.

Taurasi added five rebounds and a career NCAA Tournament-high nine assists.

But Taurasi almost wasn't needed. She scored all but two of her points in the final 23 minutes, after UConn had built a 42-19 lead.

"If we don't get Diana involved then it's not good for us, because that's what makes it go for us," coach Geno Auriemma said. "But at the same time if it's all Diana, all the time, the other kids don't get the opportunity to assert themselves. We're Connecticut. We're not Diana and the others. We're Connecticut."

Ann Strother had 10 points for UConn. Jewel Clark, the Ivy League Player of the Year, led Penn (17-11) with 16 points but spent most of the night in foul trouble trying to guard Turner.

Clark got off to a slow start with Taurasi hounding her on defense. Clark missed her first two shots—the second an air ball from the wing—then picked up her first foul trying to stop Turner in the post.

Turner made one of two free throws, then posted Clark a second time for a turnaround jumper and scored

		1st	2nd	Total
Pennsylvania		23	32	55
UConn		51	40	91

Penn

Player	FGM-A	3PM-A	FTM-A	O-D REB	A	BLK	S	TP
20 J. Clark	5-16	0-2	6-6	4-1	0	0	1	16
54 J. Fleisher	2-3	0-0	0-0	1-9	0	0	1	4
12 A. Kammes	0-3	0-0	0-0	1-0	3	0	0	0
22 M. Austin	5-14	4-7	0-0	1-3	2	0	1	14
44 K. Habrukowich	0-4	0-1	1-2	0-0	4	0	0	1
04 L. Pears	1-1	0-0	0-0	0-1	0	0	0	2
11 J. Rhoads	1-6	1-3	0-0	0-2	2	0	1	3
14 M. Didonato	1-2	1-2	0-0	0-0	0	0	1	3
23 C. Makarewich	0-2	0-1	0-0	1-1	0	0	0	0
24 A. Gray	0-0	0-0	0-0	0-1	2	0	0	0
32 H. Hansen	0-0	0-0	0-0	0-0	0	0	0	0
33 J. Hosenbold	0-0	0-0	0-0	0-0	0	0	0	0
42 M. Naltner	0-4	0-0	0-0	0-1	1	0	1	0
43 J. Markoff	0-0	0-0	0-0	0-0	0	0	0	0
51 K. Kilker	6-8	0-0	0-1	3-1	0	0	0	12

UConn

Player	FGM-A	3PM-A	FTM-A	O-D REB	A	BLK	S	TP
33 B. Turner	7-14	1-4	2-4	0-2	3	0	0	17
43 A. Strother	4-9	0-3	2-2	3-3	2	0	0	10
31 J. Moore	6-9	0-0	3-4	3-8	0	0	0	15
03 D. Taurasi	6-11	4-7	2-2	0-5	9	0	0	18
05 M. Conlon	1-4	1-3	0-0	1-4	2	0	1	3
02 A. Valley	1-1	1-1	3-4	1-1	1	0	2	6
04 K. Robinson	1-3	0-1	0-2	0-0	0	0	1	2
12 S. Marron	0-0	0-0	2-2	0-0	0	0	0	2
20 M. Valley	1-1	0-0	0-0	2-2	2	0	2	2
22 A. Battle	3-3	0-0	3-4	1-1	2	0	4	9
23 W. Crockett	1-1	0-0	3-4	0-2	2	0	1	5
34 L. Sherwood	1-3	0-0	0-0	0-0	0	3	0	2

on an offensive rebound to give UConn a 15-6 lead with 12:50 left.

The Huskies led 19-10 when Moore and Turner sparked a 10-2 run. Turner scored on a feed from Ashley Battle to make it 29-12 with 7:09 left.

"I'm glad we won because we played well, not because we're just a better team," Auriemma said. "The only chance Penn had tonight was if we played poorly, and we didn't play poorly."

THREE FOR ALL

By Jeff Goldberg *The Hartford Courant*

Auburn used a zone. UConn was in one. The Huskies played as close to perfection as they have all season in the second round of the NCAA Tournament, combining equal parts suffocating defense and free-wheeling offense. The Huskies nearly pitched a shutout in the second half, holding Auburn without a field goal for the first 16:11. At the other end, the Huskies bombed away against Auburn's vaunted matchup zone, shooting their way back to Hartford with a 79-53 victory before 9,091 at the Arena at Harbor Yard.

By the time it was over, UConn had tied a school record with 14 three-pointers and Auburn had tied an East Regional record for futility with 18 field goals.

"Wow," said UConn coach Geno Auriemma, who celebrated his 50th birthday. "I thought we did the best job we have done all season, and I'm really proud of them and their effort. Sometimes it evolves right in front of you. Everything we had planned came to fruition. The players made it happen."

The Huskies are two games from reaching a record fifth straight Final Four. It is the 11th straight season UConn has reached the round of 16.

Diana Taurasi, who was named Naismith Player of the Year and Associated Press first-team All-American for the second consecutive season, hit five of nine three-pointers and scored 17 points, moving into third place on the NCAA Tournament's all-time scoring list with 345. Her seven assists left her one shy of tying Jennifer Rizzotti's school record of 637.

Ann Strother made four of eight threes and had 16 points. Maria Conlon also made four of eight and tied her NCAA Tournament career high with 12 points.

"They were doubling inside, and our spacing was really good," Strother said. "We had a lot of open outside shots, and they were going in tonight."

But it was a second half of defensive brilliance by a UConn team that has relied on its defense all season that put the game away. UConn led 42-36 at the half, but Auburn missed its first 17 shots over 16 minutes.

By the time Le'Coe Willingham (16 points) scored with 3:49 left, UConn had a 72-40 lead, opening the half with a 30-4 run.

OPPOSITE: Diana Taurasi hugs Maria Conlon as Conlon walks off the court. Conlon finished with 12 points and four assists. Taurasi added with 17 points and seven assists in the Huskies' convincing 26-point win over the Auburn University Tigers. *Michael McAndrews/The Hartford Courant*

ABOVE: Barbara Turner celebrates as the Huskies move forward to the next round of the tournament.
Michael McAndrews/The Hartford Courant

UConn made its 14 three-pointers on 27 attempts. It tied the East Regional record for most three-pointers in a game and busted the previous school NCAA record of 11 against Long Island in the 2001 first round.

"Throughout the season, I've been trying to get a handle on who we are and what we're about," Auriemma said. "Were we the kind of team that could dig in, play defense and rebound against a team a little bigger and stronger? Were we the kind of team that could execute offensively, run our stuff with a bit of patience and still be aggressive at the same time? I thought tonight we did a better job of those two things at the same time in so far the biggest game of the year."

UConn blew open the game to start the second half, scoring the first 10 points to take a 52-36 lead with 15:48 left. The run consisted of long and short baskets, with Jessica Moore making a pair of hook shots between three-pointers by Maria Conlon and Diana Taurasi. A three by Taurasi that capped the run was UConn's 10th of the game.

"I think Jess made the biggest difference in the second half," Taurasi said. "Her couple of buckets inside really took the air out of them."

UConn centered its attack by going to Barbara Turner (13 points) early, getting the sophomore forward open on the Huskies' first two possessions for scores. From there, the Huskies looked exclusively for the three-point shot, making five of six in the first seven minutes to take a 21-15 lead.

	1st	2nd	Total
Auburn	36	17	53
UConn	42	37	79

Auburn

Player	FGM-A	3PM-A	FTM-A	O-D REB	A	BLK	S	TP
43 L. Willingham	6-8	1-2	3-5	0-4	0	1	1	16
54 M. Stevenson	2-10	2-4	0-0	2-3	1	0	0	6
11 N. Louden	1-5	0-2	0-0	0-1	4	0	1	2
12 N. Derrick	0-0	0-0	0-0	1-0	1	0	0	0
33 N. Brackett	2-9	1-4	4-6	1-2	1	0	1	9
03 N. Brown	2-8	1-5	1-2	0-0	1	0	4	6
10 M. Payne	0-1	0-0	2-2	0-1	1	1	0	2
14 L. Emeagi	5-9	2-4	0-0	4-0	1	1	2	12
21 T. Presley	0-0	0-0	0-0	0-0	1	0	0	0

UConn

Player	FGM-A	3PM-A	FTM-A	O-D REB	A	BLK	S	TP
02 A. Valley	1-1	1-1	0-0	0-0	0	0	0	3
03 D. Taurasi	6-12	5-9	0-0	0-3	7	0	0	17
04 K. Robinson	0-0	0-0	2-2	0-1	0	0	0	2
05 M. Conlon	4-8	4-8	0-0	0-0	4	1	0	12
12 S. Marron	0-0	0-0	0-0	0-0	0	0	0	0
20 M. Valley	1-1	0-0	0-0	0-1	0	0	0	2
22 A. Battle	2-2	0-0	0-0	0-4	2	0	0	4
23 W. Crockett	0-1	0-0	2-4	3-2	0	0	0	2
31 J. Moore	4-5	0-0	0-0	2-2	0	1	2	8
33 B. Turner	6-13	0-1	1-1	3-3	6	2	4	13
34 L. Sherwood	0-1	0-0	0-0	1-0	0	0	0	0
43 A. Strother	6-10	4-8	0-0	0-5	4	0	0	16

UConn nailed eight of its first 10 threes and led 35-27 with 4:24 left in the half.

"We played a great team tonight, a team that showed why it's the defending champion," Auburn coach Joe Ciampi said. "If they play like this throughout the tournament, great things will happen for them."

IT'S UC NOT UCSB

Willnett Crockett and UC Santa Barbara's Lisa Willett chase down a rebound in the second half. UConn won 63-55.
Michael McAndrews/The Hartford Courant

UCONN 63 | UC SANTA BARBARA 55

ROUGH RIDE FOR HUSKIES

By Jeff Goldberg *The Hartford Courant*

She was bounced, bruised, bloodied and bowed. But Diana Taurasi and UConn were not beaten. Cinderella wore brass knuckles on her final night at the big dance, but it was the Huskies who were standing at the final bell. UConn, the No. 2 seed in the East Regional, answered every challenge from No. 11 UC Santa Barbara, holding on for a 63-55 victory before 14,253 at the Civic Center to reach the regional final.

But it was not until the final 46 seconds, when the Huskies made eight of ten free throws to push a five-point lead to 11, that UConn could finally celebrate its 10th appearance in the Elite Eight in the past 11 years.

"In a game like this where you're not going to get a call and nothing is really going your way for the whole game, our composure and poise came out at the end," Taurasi said.

Taurasi, who passed Jen Rizzotti to become UConn's all-time assists leader, led the Huskies with 21 points. Against perhaps the most physical opponent UConn has faced this season, Taurasi struggled for the first 33 minutes, taking a hard shot to the ribs and cutting her left knee in the first half, then falling into a one-for-10 shooting slump in the second.

But with the Huskies clinging to a 45-39 lead with 7:07 left, Taurasi caught fire, hitting back-to-back jumpers for a 10-point lead. Then, with UConn up seven and less than two minutes left, Taurasi stole the ball from April McDivitt and hit a tough step-back jumper from the top of the key with 1:18 left to put the Huskies up, 53-44.

"I would say it's Diana's tournament so far," said Maria Conlon, whose steal and timeout with 43.6 seconds left was the back breaker. "They were really physical with her the whole game. She wasn't making as many shots as she wanted, but she did a good job of keeping her composure, and it just shows the leadership she carries."

The Huskies are now 40 minutes from history. On the same day the UConn men advanced to the Final Four for the second time, the Huskies gave themselves the chance to become the first women's team to reach five straight Final Fours.

RIGHT: UConn's Diana Taurasi does her best Michael Jordan imitation, sticking her tongue out after hitting a big shot late in the NCAA East Regional semifinal game at the Hartford Civic Center. Taurasi led UConn with 21 points.

Bob MacDonnell/The Hartford Courant

SWEET SIXTEEN | MARCH 27, 2004

UConn 63 | UC Santa Barbara 55

UConn (28-4) can do it with a victory over top-seeded Penn State in the regional final. The Lady Lions (28-5) advanced with a 55-49 victory over No. 5 Notre Dame.

Jessica Moore, who helped hold Santa Barbara's six-foot-eight center, Lindsay Taylor, to a season-low five points, had her second double-double in three games with 10 points and 10 rebounds.

Ashley Battle made perhaps the biggest shot of the game, a three-pointer with 11:16 left to start the Huskies on a 9-0 run for a 45-34 lead. Battle came in with only five three-pointers on 13 attempts this season.

"That was a huge three," Conlon said. "Sometimes she doesn't look for that shot. She should, more. That was huge. Everybody else just kind of fed off that."

McDivitt, the former Tennessee Lady Vol, led Santa Barbara with 20 points, including five three-pointers.

UConn's 63 points were its lowest total in an NCAA Tournament game since scoring 58 in a 1999 Mideast Regional semifinal against Iowa State. That was the last year UConn failed to reach the Final Four.

UConn struggled against a physical and aggressive Santa Barbara defense that forced the Huskies to play faster than they wanted. Several times in the first half, UConn coach Geno Auriemma implored his team to slow down, to no avail.

"Artistically, it was not a masterpiece," he said. "It was a pretty great win. The shots were really hard to

				1st	2nd	Total
UC Santa Barbara				22	33	55
UConn				28	35	63

UC Santa Barbara

Player	FGM-A	3PM-A	FTM-A	O-D REB	A	BLK	S	TP
15 B. Richardson	1-3	0-1	3-3	2-4	2	0	3	5
44 K. Mann	5-19	0-5	2-2	2-3	0	0	2	12
13 L. Taylor	2-11	0-1	1-2	1-6	0	1	0	5
10 A. McDivitt	6-12	5-10	3-6	0-1	3	0	4	20
21 M. Fisher	0-4	0-0	0-0	2-0	2	0	1	0
14 L. Willett	2-5	2-4	0-0	1-1	0	0	0	6
22 E. O'Bryan	1-1	1-1	0-0	0-0	0	0	0	3
32 K. Bonds	1-2	0-0	0-0	3-0	1	0	0	2
33 J. Green	1-2	0-0	0-0	1-1	0	0	1	2

UConn

Player	FGM-A	3PM-A	FTM-A	O-D REB	A	BLK	S	TP
33 B. Turner	3-8	0-1	7-8	4-1	4	0	1	13
43 A. Strother	3-7	2-4	0-0	0-2	2	1	1	8
31 J. Moore	4-8	0-0	2-6	3-7	1	2	0	10
03 D. Taurasi	9-21	1-9	2-2	2-3	4	0	2	21
05 M. Conlon	1-7	1-6	3-4	0-3	1	0	3	6
20 M. Valley	0-0	0-0	0-0	0-0	0	0	0	0
22 A. Battle	1-2	1-1	2-2	2-6	0	0	1	5
23 W. Crockett	0-0	0-0	0-0	1-2	1	1	1	0

come by. ... I think our players showed what they're made of in the last five minutes."

The Gauchos refused to wilt. Their last gasp came with 48.8 seconds left, when Brandy Richardson stole the ball from Taurasi under the Gauchos basket and made a three-point play to cut UConn's lead to 55-50.

But the Huskies made the big plays at the end. Turner hit both ends of a one-and-one, then Conlon stole Kristen Mann's inbounds pass and called timeout before falling out of bounds. Conlon made two free throws for a 59-50 lead with 40.1 seconds left.

OPPOSITE: Maria Conlon calls for a timeout as she goes out of bounds after she stole the ball from a Santa Barbara inbounds play in the second half. *Michael McAndrews/The Hartford Courant*

T PARTY

Diana Taurasi, who finished with 27 points, welcomes to
the bench in the closing seconds Barbara Turner, who finished with 26 points, as UConn advances to its fifth consecutive Final Four. *Michael McAndrews/The Hartford Courant*

NEW ORLEANS BOUND

By Jeff Goldberg *The Hartford Courant*

UConn officially has a dynasty. And dynasty starts with D.

The Huskies now stand alone in the history of women's college basketball, reaching an unprecedented fifth consecutive Final Four with a 66-49 victory over Penn State in the NCAA Tournament East Regional final at the Civic Center. It was a crowning moment for Diana Taurasi. The East Regional's Most Outstanding Player scored 27 points, including six in a 9-0 run that stopped a second-half Penn State rally.

"It's just an unbelievable feeling,"Taurasi said. "If you try to put it into words, it kind of takes away from it. It couldn't have played out any better. This has been a hard year, but this is great."

Taurasi was not a one-woman show on this night. Sophomore Barbara Turner, one of the players who will lead the Huskies into the post-Taurasi era, scored 26 points, hitting a career-high four three-pointers. They combined for 53 of UConn's 66 points.

Turner scored eight straight points early in the second half and 11 of 14 as the Huskies built a 47-26 lead with 11:56 left.

And when the Lady Lions cut the lead to nine with 7:20 left, Taurasi and Turner turned them back. Taurasi, who moved into second place on the all-time NCAA Tournament scoring list (393 points), hit a three-pointer from the corner to push UConn's lead back to 54-42. Then, after Taurasi made two free throws for a 14-point lead, Turner hit her fourth three-pointer for a 59-42 lead with 5:20 left.

Taurasi made a free throw, and the Huskies bled the clock, leading by at least 14 for the final four minutes.

"I just think we were tougher,"Taurasi said. "In the second half, when they made their run, we could have easily folded. But we came back and made some plays. When you get this far, it's just how tough you are and how much you don't want to go home, and this team does not want to go home."

OPPOSITE: **Barbara Turner tries to pump up the crowd after going on a tear to open the second half during the NCAA East Regional final game between UConn and Penn State at the Hartford Civic Center. Turner scored 26 points, with a career-high four three-pointers.** *Bob MacDonnell/The Hartford Courant*

And as the final two minutes ticked down on the final game in Connecticut this season, the crowd of 14,855 showered seniors Taurasi, Maria Conlon and Morgan Valley and the rest of the Huskies with a thunderous ovation, loud enough to launch them to New Orleans.

The trio of seniors joins four other players in NCAA women's history—all from Tennessee—as the only ones to reach the Final Four in all four years.

"You always hope that for some of your seniors, fairy tales end with a happy ending," Auriemma said. "I was hoping and praying that today wouldn't be their last game, that they would have the opportunity to go back to the Final Four, because as a senior that's the culmination of your career."

Penn State's Kelly Mazzante, the ninth leading scorer in NCAA history with 2,919 points, had 14 on five-for-17 shooting. Tanisha Wright led the Lady Lions with 16 but also shot five for 17.

UConn held top-seeded Penn State to a season-low 13 points in the first half, limiting Mazzante to two points on one-for-seven shooting. But the Lady Lions did not go quietly.

They held two UConn starters, Conlon and Ann Strother, scoreless. And after UConn took a 47-26 lead with 11:56 left and appeared to have the game wrapped up, Mazzante led a 16-3 run to close to 51-42 with 7:20 left.

Then Taurasi and Turner ended it.

"This is not a fun way to end a season," Penn State coach Rene Portland said. "[UConn] came out with a

		1st	2nd	Total
UConn		21	45	66
Penn State		13	36	49

UConn

Player	FGM-A	3PM-A	FTM-A	O-D REB	A	BLK	S	TP
33 B. Turner	8-11	4-5	6-10	3-3	3	0	0	26
31 J. Moore	3-5	0-0	2-2	0-7	2	2	2	8
03 D. Taurasi	8-15	2-7	9-12	0-5	3	0	1	27
05 M. Conlon	0-2	0-1	0-0	0-2	3	0	1	0
43 A. Strother	0-5	0-4	0-0	1-5	0	2	0	0
02 A. Valley	0-0	0-0	1-2	0-0	0	0	0	1
20 M. Valley	0-0	0-0	0-0	0-0	0	0	0	0
22 A. Battle	1-3	0-1	0-0	1-0	1	0	2	2
23 W. Crockett	1-1	0-0	0-0	1-6	0	3	0	2

Penn State

Player	FGM-A	3PM-A	FTM-A	O-D REB	A	BLK	S	TP
22 J. Brungo	2-10	2-5	0-2	3-2	0	0	1	6
50 R. Russell	1-1	0-0	0-0	2-2	0	2	1	2
13 K. Mazzante	5-17	1-8	3-3	1-3	2	0	0	14
23 J. Strom	1-10	1-5	1-2	0-3	2	0	2	4
33 T. Wright	5-17	0-0	6-6	1-0	2	0	1	16
15 A. Brown	1-1	0-0	0-0	2-4	0	0	1	2
51 A. Schwab	0-0	0-0	0-0	0-0	0	0	0	0
53 J. Harris	1-1	1-1	2-2	1-0	0	0	0	5

great effort. We obviously didn't have an answer for Barbara Turner, and we'll go home wondering."

Now these Huskies, doubted by many entering the NCAA Tournament after their first four-loss season since the year before the Final Four streak began, can become the second team, along with the 1996-98 Lady Vols, to win three straight championships.

"I don't know how the story is going to end next weekend, because there's still another chapter to be written," Auriemma said. "But as far as the Connecticut version of the fairy tale, that ended exactly the way I hoped it would end."

OPPOSITE: Diana Taurasi splits the defense of Jessica Brungo (left) and Jennifer Harris. *Bob MacDonnell/The Hartford Courant*

Diana Taurasi leaves the Civic Center wearing her uniform after the Huskies beat Penn State 66-49 to advance to the school's fifth consecutive Final Four, a record streak.
Michael McAndrews/The Hartford Courant

BIG SHOTS

Diana Taurasi tries in vain to block Janel McCarville. McCarville scored 18 points inside, but UConn's defense held the Gophers' other star, Lindsay Whalen, to 11 points as they beat Minnesota 67-58 to advance to the championship game. *Bob MacDonnell/The Hartford Courant*

UCONN TURNS BACK MINNESOTA

By Jeff Goldberg *The Hartford Courant*

Ann Strother was standing upright in the locker room, but just barely. Her face was flush, her arms limp.

She had just been in the battle of her basketball life. But she survived. UConn survived.

It has been the Year of the Underdog in women's basketball, a season where the No. 1 ranking acted like Kryptonite and upsets ruled the NCAA Tournament.

The Final Four featured two new teams, one seeded fourth, the other seventh. At last, parity had come to rule women's basketball.

Well, almost.

The more things change, the more it's UConn and Tennessee in the championship game.

The Huskies printed their invitation to history, holding off determined, upstart Minnesota 67-58 in the national semifinals before 18,211 at New Orleans Arena.

It was a game that lived up to its advance billing, with the seventh-seeded Golden Gophers taking every UConn punch and fighting right back, trailing by two points until the final six minutes, when the Huskies finally wrestled free into the title game.

"I was telling Stacey [Marron] that was the most emotional game I've played in," said Strother, whose three-pointer with 3:24 left was the shot that finally pierced Minnesota's stout heart. "We jump on them, they come back. It's trading baskets until the last six minutes. Whew. We're emotionally exhausted."

After a season with four losses and infinite questions about their dynastic hold on the sport, the Huskies are one victory from becoming the second team in Division I history to win three straight championships.

The only team to accomplish that is Tennessee (1996-98), and after a heart-stopping 52-50 victory over LSU in the first semifinal, UConn's old buddies from Knoxville will seek to keep it that way.

Minnesota, the No. 7 seed out of the Mideast, got to this game by making run after run against Duke in the regional final. They were back at it against UConn in the second half Sunday, twice going on 7-0 runs to cut the deficit to two, the last with 6:07 left.

OPPOSITE: Barbara Turner shoots over Janel McCarville. Turner was held to seven points, but UConn beat Minnesota 67-58 to advance to the championship game against Tennessee. *Bob MacDonnell/The Hartford Courant*

RIGHT: UConn gathers on the court to celebrate as the Huskies advance to the finals. *Michael McAndrews/The Hartford Courant*

But UConn had the final answer, going on a 10-4 run to take a 63-55 lead with 2:37 left.

"That was one of the best teams I've played since I've been here, four years," UConn's Diana Taurasi said. "They weren't going to give up. They made it this far, and they were going to fight and crawl until the last seconds."

Taurasi led the Huskies with 18 points, giving her 2,139 for her career, two short of third in UConn history. Maria Conlon had 10 for the Huskies (30-4) and Willnett Crockett had nine off the bench, including four in UConn's final push.

Janel McCarville led Minnesota (25-9) with 18 points. Lindsay Whalen had 11.

"It's funny how everything comes full-circle," Taurasi said. "When I came in as a freshman, it was always Connecticut-Tennessee. You're going to love playing in those games. I'm a senior now and it's Tennessee for a national championship. It's going to be a battle."

UConn led 37-29 at the half Sunday, when the Minnesota cheering section picked up a chant of "We Believe" as the second half began. And the Golden Gophers had reason to believe when Whalen scored on a drive with 17:48 left to cut UConn's lead to 39-35.

But as was the theme of this game, UConn responded with a 7-0 run for an 11-point lead, only to see Minnesota charge right back with a 9-0 run, including six points by McCarville, to make it 46-44.

Taurasi hit a three to start a 7-0 UConn run, then back came the Gophers, scoring another seven in a row to close to 53-51 with 7:34 left.

But Barbara Turner rebounded a Conlon miss and converted a three-point play for a five-point lead.

	1st	2nd	Total
Minnesota	29	29	58
UConn	37	30	67

Minnesota

PLAYER	FGM-A	3PTM-A	FTM-A	O-D REB	A	BK	S	PTS
22 S. Bolden	1-5	1-3	1-2	0-1	1	0	0	4
35 K. Andersson	2-4	0-0	0-1	3-1	2	0	0	4
04 J. McCarville	8-13	0-0	2-2	1-6	3	1	4	18
11 S. Schonrock	3-8	3-8	0-0	0-0	1	0	1	9
13 L. Whalen	3-11	0-3	5-6	2-4	7	0	1	11
03 K. Roysland	1-1	0-0	0-1	0-0	0	0	0	2
33 J. Broback	4-8	2-3	0-0	1-3	1	0	3	10
55 L. Podominick	0-0	0-0	0-0	0-0	0	0	0	0

UConn

PLAYER	FGM-A	3PTM-A	FTM-A	O-D REB	A	BK	S	PTS
33 B. Turner	3-7	0-1	1-1	3-1	2	1	1	7
31 J. Moore	3-4	0-0	0-0	3-5	1	1	1	6
03 D. Taurasi	6-17	2-7	4-5	0-6	3	3	0	18
05 M. Conlon	4-7	2-5	0-0	0-4	1	0	2	10
43 A. Strother	4-7	1-3	0-0	1-3	1	1	0	9
22 A. Battle	2-4	0-1	4-4	2-3	1	0	2	8
23 W. Crockett	4-8	0-0	1-2	3-0	1	0	3	9

UConn's lead was 58-55 with 5:50 left when the Huskies committed turnovers on three straight possessions. But Minnesota missed shots each time, and after Whalen missed on the Gophers' fourth chance to close to one, Strother hit her three-pointer to give UConn a 61-55 lead with 3:24 left.

Then Taurasi found Crockett for a layup with 2:37 left and an eight-point lead.

"I can't put into words the admiration that I feel for the kids from Minnesota," UConn coach Geno Auriemma said. "To beat them today is as gratifying as anything we've ever done at the University of Connecticut."

Minnesota's Jamie Broback (at left) and Janel McCarville hide their tears after losing to UConn in the Final Four.
Bob MacDonnell/The Hartford Courant

MAKE IT THREE IN A ROW

A victorious UConn team hoists the national championship trophy after beating Tennessee 70-61. *Michael McAndrews/The Hartford Courant*

TAURASI CAPS CAREER WITH ANOTHER TITLE

By Jeff Goldberg *The Hartford Courant*

On Selection Sunday, UConn coach Geno Auriemma reflected on an arduous regular season.

The Huskies had lost four games—a rarity in the past few seasons—and players and coaches alike conceded they sometimes lacked the focus and intensity needed to win a third straight championship.

"The journey the first time you go to the beach is fun as a kid," Auriemma said that day. "The next couple of years, you just want to get to the water. You don't want to deal with the car ride."

But what a ride this tournament has been. And in the final, the Huskies bathed themselves in glory.

UConn became the second team in Division I women's basketball history to win three straight national championships, gutting out a 70-61 victory over Tennessee before 18,211 at New Orleans Arena.

"There's a tremendous amount of responsibility that the kids carry around," Auriemma said. "And I think it got to them this year. All we had to do was focus on three weekends in March, because the journey leading up to that was very, very hard. They had to defend it

every night. It's hard to do that. It's just remarkable what they were able to do, under the circumstances."

The Lady Vols had been the only team to win three straight titles. But the Huskies continued the assault on their archrivals' stranglehold on the record book, winning the fifth title in program history—all in the past 10 seasons—leaving UConn one shy of Tennessee's total.

"It's history," Diana Taurasi said. "I think being from the University of Connecticut, we always think of ourselves as a basketball school, and this year we made a definite impact on how prominent our programs are."

Taurasi ends her career with 2,156 points, third most all-time at UConn, and the championship left little doubt as to her place as the greatest player in UConn history.

"It's been amazing," Taurasi said. "Coming in as a freshman, I never expected this at all. I know I speak for

OPPOSITE: Diana Taurasi scores two points over Tennessee's Shyra Ely during the first half of the championship game. Taurasi had 17 points and was named the tournament's **Most Outstanding Player.** *Bob MacDonnell/The Hartford Courant*

RIGHT: Barbara Turner muscles her way in for a layup under Ashley Robinson. Turner finished the game with 12 points. *Michael McAndrews/The Hartford Courant*

UConn 70 | Tennessee 61

[seniors] Maria [Conlon] and Morgan [Valley], it's just unbelievable. Three in a row? You just don't do that."

But the true hero of this championship night was center Jessica Moore, who scored 12 of her 14 points in the second half to prevent UConn from wilting under a furious Tennessee charge.

Moore twisted her right knee grabbing an offensive rebound with 6:26 left and had to leave the game for several minutes. But that rebound led to three Ann Strother free throws and an eight-point lead. Tennessee got no closer than four the rest of the way.

"I was thinking in my head, there was no way we were going to lose," said Moore, who had nine rebounds. "And I was going to do anything I could to help us win."

But like just about everything this season, this final victory did not come easy. It appeared it might with 6:29 left in the first half, when Strother hit UConn's fifth three-pointer for a 30-13 lead. But UConn went cold, and Tennessee scored the last 11 points of the half to cut the lead to six. Then Zolman hit a jumper to open the second half to make it 30-26.

But Moore kept UConn afloat, scoring the Huskies' first eight points of the half, the last on a pick-and-roll from Conlon that offset a five-point burst by Zolman to put UConn ahead, 38-33.

Moore then drew a charge on LaToya Davis, and Taurasi cashed in the possession with a three-pointer for an eight-point lead.

The Lady Vols, who showed true grit in three games to reach the final, kept coming, closing to 48-45, then 50-48 with 9:51 to go with Taurasi on the bench getting a rest.

				1st	2nd	Total
UConn				30	40	70
Tennessee				24	37	61

UConn

PLAYER	FGM-A	3PTM-A	FTM-A	O-D REB	A	BK	S	PTS
33 B. Turner	4-12	1-2	3-6	1-8	4	2	2	12
31 J. Moore	6-9	0-0	2-2	6-3	1	0	2	14
03 D. Taurasi	6-11	3-7	2-4	0-3	2	0	0	17
05 M. Conlon	1-4	1-2	4-4	0-2	5	0	2	7
43 A. Strother	5-8	1-2	3-3	0-2	2	0	0	14
22 A. Battle	1-4	1-1	0-0	0-1	0	0	1	3
23 W. Crockett	1-3	0-0	1-1	0-2	1	0	0	3

Tennessee

PLAYER	FGM-A	3PTM-A	FTM-A	O-D REB	A	BK	S	PTS
04 L. Davis	3-8	0-0	0-0	1-0	7	0	4	6
43 S. Ely	4-10	0-0	2-4	2-5	0	0	0	10
33 A. Robinson	6-10	0-0	1-4	4-3	1	2	0	13
03 T. Butts	1-10	0-6	6-6	3-3	2	0	3	8
05 S. Zolman	6-11	3-6	4-4	2-7	1	0	1	19
01 S. Spencer	0-1	0-0	0-0	0-1	0	0	0	0
13 D. Redding	0-1	0-0	0-0	0-0	1	0	0	0
25 B. Jackson	1-7	1-4	0-0	0-1	1	0	0	3
50 T. Fluker	1-3	0-0	0-0	1-0	0	0	0	2

Moore scored inside to put UConn up four, and Strother posted up Brittany Jackson to make it 54-48. Then came Moore's rebound and injury and Strother's three free throws, followed soon after by Crockett's three-point play.

Tennessee came back one final time, cutting it to 62-57 with 2:22 left. But seniors Taurasi and Conlon each hit two free throws on consecutive possessions to put UConn up nine with 1:32 left.

The title was theirs.

"They have a toughness about them," Summitt said. "An aggressiveness and obviously a confidence. I think they obviously get that from their coach. I thought Diana brought that as well. I have a lot of respect for Geno, and I have a lot of respect for this Connecticut program."

PASSING THE TORCH

By Lori Riley *The Hartford Courant*

Maria Conlon stood on the podium in the middle of the court at New Orleans Arena. She did not smile. She did not yell "Jubilations!" into a microphone. She was too busy blinking away tears.

"I felt like a big baby," the UConn senior guard said after the Huskies won their third consecutive national title. "I was thinking, 'This is it. This is great. This is unreal. Who ends their career like this?' That's why I couldn't speak. It was just an unreal moment. It was my last time playing with Barbara, Ann, Jess and AB and everybody.

"I feel like it was just yesterday that we were in St. Louis [in the 2001 Final Four] in the locker room, crying our eyes out, saying we never wanted to have this feeling again. And sure enough, we never did. We're really fortunate."

UConn won its fifth title, fourth in the past five years. The juniors won their third in as many years. Next year, they pick up the burden to carry on the legacy seniors Diana Taurasi, Morgan Valley and Conlon helped continue. Next year's Huskies will need a new point guard. A new go-to player. A new emotional leader.

Last season, the underclassmen, still leaning heavily on Taurasi, might not have been up to such a challenge. But this season was a little bit different. Taurasi, who finished 22 points shy of UConn's career scoring record, third behind Nykesha Sales and Kerry Bascom, was not as dominant. Barbara Turner scored more. Everybody else contributed and kicked up their defense a few notches. It was a team effort. And, as part of the maturation process, UConn lost four times.

"The only question they asked themselves was, 'What more do I have to do to help this team win?'" UConn associate head coach Chris Dailey said. "And that starts with D. She was more demanding of them this year. She helped them raise their game to another level. That's the great thing about [Tuesday's] game. We didn't force it to her. Everyone stepped up.

"Last year, it was, 'We've got Diana, and you don't.' This year, it was, 'We're Connecticut, and you're not.'"

That attitude was evident in the NCAA Tournament. Jessica Moore averaged 10.1 points and 8.1 rebounds in

OPPOSITE: Ann Strother drives past Tye'sha Fluker. Strother's 14 points helped UConn nab a third consecutive national championship. *Bob MacDonnell/The Hartford Courant*

six NCAA games. Turner, who had averaged 4.6 rebounds in the NCAAs before Tuesday, had nine rebounds against Tennessee. She averaged 15.2 points in six NCAA games after averaging 13.7 during the season.

"We've got to learn to play without [the seniors]," Moore said. "We've got a lot of work to do."

That's one reason why the seniors aren't worried that their legacy won't be carried on.

Conlon was asked after the game if the younger players will be OK.

"Oh yeah," she said breezily. "We've got Barbara Turner. Jessica Moore, Ann Strother. There's just something about this program, you know? This is the feeling you want every year. There's no way that these guys aren't fired up to get back again next year."

Moore and Battle will be fifth-year seniors providing leadership. Strother and Turner, entering their junior

year, will score; Strother will likely help out in the backcourt. Nicole Wolff should return from her ACL injury and, if she is healthy, can play point guard, as can incoming freshman Mel Thomas. And Charde Houston, the six-foot-one forward from San Diego who broke Cheryl Miller's California high school scoring record, could start. Willnett Crockett, who also will be a junior, will likely provide a boost off the bench.

"I think we all have it in us," Crockett said. "If we carry on the tradition—you go in there, you fight for 40 minutes and you get the job done, no matter what happens, we'll be fine.

"We don't want to be the class that doesn't get the job done. We've got to come in and work hard, knowing that we're going to lose a lot of key players on our team. I think we're willing and ready to take that chance. I'm ready for it."

"Last year, it was, 'We've got Diana, and you don't.' This year, it was, 'We're Connecticut, and you're not.'"
—Chris Dailey

OPPOSITE: Diana Taurasi's teammates mob her after the final buzzer sounds. *Bob MacDonnell/The Hartford Courant*

Diana Taurasi waves her snippet of the net during the postgame ceremonies.
Michael McAndrews/The Hartford Courant

Season Results

Date	Opponent	Site	Result
Nov. 8	Team Concept (exhibition)	Storrs, CT	W 79-59
Nov. 18	NWBL All-Stars (exhibition)	Hartford, CT	W 96-51
Nov. 23	Western Michigan	Storrs, CT	W 95-46
Nov. 25	Florida State	Hartford, CT	W 81-53
Nov. 30	Holy Cross	Hartford, CT	W 76-42
Dec. 2	Siena	Storrs, CT	W 69-45
Dec. 5	Pepperdine	Malibu, CA	W 84-53
Dec. 7	Southern California	Los Angeles, CA	W 72-69
Dec. 18	Arizona State	Hartford, CT	W 81-55
Dec. 21	St. Joseph's	Philadelphia, PA	W 87-34
Dec. 29	North Carolina State	Hartford, CT	W 87-53
Jan. 3	Duke	Hartford, CT	L 67-68
Jan. 7	West Virginia	Morgantown, WV	W 82-57
Jan. 10	Georgetown	Storrs, CT	W 69-51
Jan. 13	Notre Dame	South Bend, IN	L 51-66
Jan. 17	Boston College	Hartford, CT	W 69-61
Jan. 19	Rutgers	Hartford, CT	W 72-47
Jan. 24	Seton Hall	South Orange, NJ	W 71-63
Jan. 27	Virginia Tech	Blacksburg, VA	W 68-51
Jan. 31	St. John's	Storrs, CT	W 82-49
Feb. 5	Tennessee	Knoxville, TN	W 81-67
Feb. 8	Miami	Storrs, CT	W 83-65
Feb. 11	Syracuse	Syracuse, NY	W 82-38
Feb. 14	Rutgers	Piscataway, NJ	W 66-43
Feb. 17	Pittsburgh	Hartford, CT	W 97-42
Feb. 21	Boston College	Chestnut Hill, MA	W 81-60
Feb. 25	Providence	Storrs, CT	W 79-38
Feb. 28	Villanova	Villanova, PA	L 56-59
Mar. 2	West Virginia (Hartford Courant/ Careerbuilder.com Senior Salute)	Storrs, CT	W 100-72
Mar. 7	vs. Virginia Tech (Big East Tournament)	Hartford, CT	W 48-34
Mar. 8	vs. Boston College (Big East Tournament)	Hartford, CT	L 70-73
Mar. 21	Pennsylvania (NCAA Tournament)	Bridgeport, CT	W 91-55
Mar. 23	Auburn (NCAA Tournament)	Bridgeport, CT	W 79-53
Mar. 27	UC Santa Barbara (NCAA Tournament)	Hartford, CT	W 63-55
Mar. 29	Penn State (NCAA Tournament)	Hartford, CT	W 66-49
Apr. 4	Minnesota (NCAA Tournament)	New Orleans, LA	W 67-58
Apr. 6	Tennessee (NCAA Tournament)	New Orleans, LA	W 70-61

2003-04 Season Statistics

	Name	GP	FG-FGA	3-PT FG-FGA	FT-FTA	Off	Def	Ast	Blk	Stl	TP	AVG
3	Diana Taurasi	35	197-432	85-218	89-112	31	108	170	27	53	568	16.2
33	Barbara Turner	35	177-330	19-47	105-158	67	100	105	14	30	478	13.7
43	Ann Strother	35	139-318	61-161	45-57	36	114	82	27	30	384	11.0
31	Jessica Moore	35	141-228	1-2	49-90	72	175	41	27	30	332	9.5
22	Ashley Battle	35	93-179	7-17	63-76	59	94	50	6	56	256	7.3
5	Maria Conlon	35	68-174	58-141	14-21	14	88	100	4	39	208	5.9
34	Liz Sherwood	25	42-72	0-0	24-43	18	28	12	19	4	108	4.3
23	Willnett Crockett	27	42-65	0-0	28-48	34	52	12	12	16	112	4.1
2	Ashley Valley	26	23-54	6-20	27-40	9	27	37	1	15	79	3.0
21	Nicole Wolff	3	4-11	0-1	1-2	1	7	2	3	0	9	3.0
20	Morgan Valley	29	24-48	3-7	9-16	27	49	38	7	19	60	2.1
4	Kiana Robinson	18	10-31	3-10	7-11	9	16	6	0	3	30	1.7
12	Stacey Marron	22	5-19	3-12	5-6	1	4	3	0	1	18	0.8

Acknowledgments

The entire staff of *The Hartford Courant* contributed to the coverage of the 2003-04 UConn women's basketball national championship season. We gratefully acknowledge the efforts of the photography and sports departments.

Sports Department

Sports editor: Jeff Otterbein

Deputy sports editors: Scott Powers, Jeff Smith

Assistant sports editors: Bill Armstrong, Paul Rosano

Copy editors: Jay Spiegel, Gary Samek, Jenn Overman, Pat Dunne, Jerry McGuire, Mike Bartolotta, Bob Clancy, Bob Campbell, Liz Flach, John Howell, Chris Reidy, Tim Castillo, Sam Ohri, Gary Gramling, Reid Walmark.

Reporters: Jeff Goldberg, Lori Riley, John Altavilla

Columnist: Jeff Jacobs

Photography Department

Photo Editors: JoEllen Black, David Grewe, Stephanie Heisler, Bruce Moyer, Sherry Peters

Photographers: Tony Bacewicz, Tom Brown, Al Chaniewski, Tia Ann Chapman, Brad Clift, Stephen Dunn, Kathy Hanley, Rick Hartford, Michael Kodas, John Long, Bob MacDonnell, Michael McAndrews, Richard Messina, Cloe Poisson, Patrick Raycraft, Marc Yves Regis I, Shana Sureck and John Woike.

Photo intern: Thomas Cordy

Photo lab staff: Emelda Alexander, Lamont Andrews, Beth Bristow, Victor Durao, Karen Lavallee and Kathy Willard

Photo department assistant: Joan Dumaine

Special thanks to Meg Dupont and John Hinze for working on this project.

Visit us online at